The Mayfield Quick View Guide
to the Internet
for Students of Sociology

VERSION 2.0

Timothy B. Gongaware
University of Nebraska, Lincoln

Jennifer Campbell Koella
University of Tennessee, Knoxville

Michael Keene
University of Tennessee, Knoxville

Mayfield Publishing Company
Mountain View, California
London • Toronto

International Standard Book Number 0-7674-2148-5

Manufactured in the United States of America
10   9   8   7   6   5   4   3   2   1

  This book is printed on recycled paper.

Mayfield Publishing Company
1280 Villa Street
Mountain View, California 94041

CONTENTS

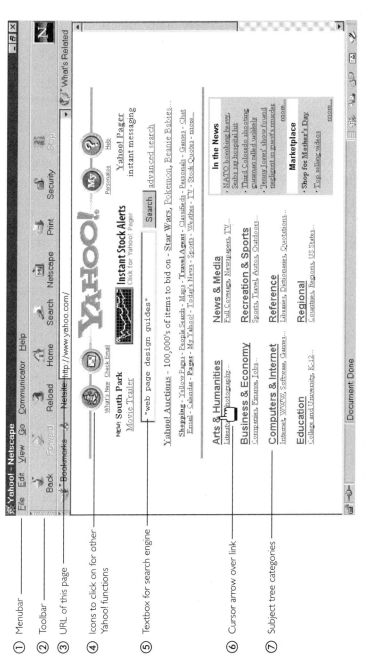

① Menubar
② Toolbar
③ URL of this page
④ Icons to click on for other Yahoo! functions
⑤ Textbox for search engine
⑥ Cursor arrow over link
⑦ Subject tree categories

Text and artwork reproduced with permission of Yahoo! Inc. copyright © 2000 by Yahoo! Inc. Yahoo! and the Yahoo! logo are trademarks of Yahoo!, Inc. Copyright © 1999 Netscape Communications Corporation. Used with permission. All rights reserved. This electronic file or page may not be reprinted or copied without the express written permission of Netscape.

INTRODUCTION

The dream behind the Web is of a common information space in which we can communicate by sharing information. Its universality is essential: the fact that a hypertext link can point to anything, be it personal, local, or global, be it draft or highly published.

—Tim Berners-Lee, "Press FAQ." 7 December 1998
<http://www.w3.org/People/Berners-Lee/FAQ.html>

What Can the Internet Do for You?

The Internet is a vast resource—not only for information, entertainment, and interaction with other people in other places who share your interests, but also for learning. You can do everything from reading newspapers and magazines, to learning how to create your own Web page, to video-conferencing, to watching video clips from your favorite movies, to down-loading free software for your computer, to taking a virtual tour of Hawaii or Frank Lloyd Wright's house, Fallingwater. The Internet often has the most current news, the best views of the weather anywhere, the best maps, and up-to-the-minute discussions of current events. Additionally, it is convenient to have a variety of dictionaries, thesauri, and encyclopedias on hand while writing a paper.

Beyond all those uses, *the Internet frees you from the physical boundaries of your hometown, your campus, your city, your state, and your country.* Information from Japan or Germany or Australia can come to you just as fast and easily as information from across the hall. Because the Internet does not have opening or closing hours, its information is more accessible than the information in your library. (And, at many schools, more and more of the library's resources are available on the Internet.) Your school's library may be tiny, but with access to the Internet, you have more information at your fingertips than the biggest library anywhere. All you need to do is learn how to find it. To help you find information on the Internet quickly—and document it correctly—is the purpose of this book.

What Are the Internet and the World Wide Web?

The Internet is a global network of computers. It is composed of many parts, such as Web documents, e-mail, Telnet, file transfer, Usenet (newsgroups), and Gopher. Until the **World Wide Web** came along, the Internet was difficult to use. *The Web is a huge number of sites of information within the Internet.*

1

Not only does the Web make accessing the Internet easier, but it also makes the Internet more fun because of the Web's **hypermedia** capabilities, such as audio, video, 3-D images, virtual reality, real-time communication, and animation. Sounds good, doesn't it? So let us help you get started!

QUICK VIEW
How Can I Use Graphic Access to the Internet?

Many students have access to computers that already have Netscape, Explorer, or some other graphic browser. If that's your situation, this page will get you off to a fast start. If you need to start from scratch, go to page 5 for more detailed directions.

Using Netscape and Other Graphic Browsers

To access the Web's multimedia capabilities, you need a graphic browser, such as Netscape or Microsoft's Internet Explorer. (*Note:* You also need TCP/IP software; see page 5.) Netscape is used in the following description; other browsers, such as Explorer, work in essentially the same way.

Click on the Netscape icon to launch the program. The first page you see will depend on your ISP (Internet service provider). Most providers have designated a Web page to appear when you start Netscape. Many people like their first screen to be a search engine, such as Yahoo! <http://www.yahoo.com>. The Netscape Help button or the Yahoo! Help button will show you how to change your start-up page. (For more customization, see your browser's Preferences section, on the View menu.)

There are several ways to access a **Web page** using Netscape. One option is to follow a **hyperlink,** which can be either text or an image. Textual hyperlinks, or **hypertext,** have a different look from the rest of the text. Depending on the browser you use, hypertext will be either a different color or underlined, or both. To follow a link, use your mouse to drag the arrow over the hypertext. When positioned over a link, the arrow will turn into a hand. Click the mouse, and you will go to that Web page. (Some links on some pages are not marked, but whenever your cursor arrow turns into a hand, you can click there and be taken somewhere else.)

Another option to clicking a link is to type out a page's address (the URL or uniform resource locator). Click on the Open button on the toolbar, type the URL in the box provided, and press Return. To navigate through a sequence of pages you have already seen, use the Back and Forward buttons on the toolbar. You may also access a Web page you have already seen by choosing it from your list of **Bookmarks,** from entries on the History list (from the Window menu), or from the Go menu.

(*Note:* URLs in this book, within the text, are enclosed in angle brackets, < >, for readability. The angle brackets are not part of the address.)

QUICK VIEW
How Can I Use Text-Only Access to the Internet?

Some students have access to computers that will give them only text from the Internet. If your computer gives you access to Lynx or some other text-only browser, this page will help you get off to a fast start. Otherwise, please turn to page 5 for more detailed instructions.

Using Lynx and Other Text-Only Browsers

Lynx is the most popular text-only browser. With text-only browsers, you cannot view the multimedia functions on the Web, such as pictures, audio, or video. You see only text. (*Note:* You do not need TCP/IP software, see page 5, to use Lynx.)

If you have a computer account at school, find out if it is a **UNIX** or **VMS** account. Chances are it will be a UNIX account. (Lynx runs on both, but our example shows how it works on UNIX.) Next, find out whether Lynx is available; if so, you can access Lynx by logging on to your computer account and then on to Lynx. After logging on, you will see either a $ or a %. Then type lynx. Your screen will look like this:

```
$ lynx
```

The first screen displayed should be a page containing information about the World Wide Web and giving you access to other pages.

To access a specific Web page, type lynx followed by the specific Web page's Internet address (its URL). For example, if you wanted to go to Netscape's home page, your command line would look like this:

```
$ lynx http://www.home.netscape.com
```

When you view a Web page, the hypertext links (shortcuts to other pages) will appear in bold. To move your cursor to a link (in bold text), use your up and down arrow keys. When you place your cursor on the bold text, the text will become highlighted. To follow the link, press the right-arrow key. To go back, press the left-arrow key.

At the bottom of the screen, you will find a list of other commands. Simply type the first letter in the command name to execute that command. When you are finished, type q to quit. You will be asked if you really want to quit; type y for yes. This will bring you back to your system prompt (the $ or the %).

(*Note:* URLs in this book, within the text, are enclosed in angle brackets, < >, for readability. The angle brackets are not part of the address.)

CHAPTER ONE
FINDING INFORMATION ON THE INTERNET

The Internet started in the 1960s as a project by the U.S. government to link supercomputers; eventually, its networking technology also came to be used by academic institutions. In the beginning, the Internet was "user hostile," and the numbers of computers and people it connected were limited. With the creation of the World Wide Web in the early 1990s by Tim Berners-Lee in Switzerland, the Internet became much more "user friendly." Today, the Internet, a global network of computers, has a great many parts: the World Wide Web, Usenet, Gopher, Telnet, and FTP (file transfer protocol).

Technically, the World Wide Web is an Internet facility that uses hypertext to link multimedia sources. Web **servers** store files that can be viewed or downloaded with a Web **browser** via **HTTP (hypertext transfer protocol)**. The most popular text-only browser is Lynx; some popular graphic browsers are Netscape, Explorer, and AOL (America Online). This book's examples use Netscape; Explorer works much the same way as Netscape.

How the Internet Works—In Brief

To find the information you want, you should know a little about how your computer works with the Internet. That is the subject of the next five brief sections. If you are not interested in learning more about how computers work, you can skip to "How to Find the Information You Want," on page 8.

Hardware and Software

To gain access to the Internet, you need a computer with the appropriate hardware and software and an **ISP (Internet service provider)**. Some popular ISPs are AOL, CompuServe, MSN, and AT&T WorldNet. To access the Internet from home, you need a computer with a **modem** to connect your computer to the phone lines. Most modems run at 28.8K or 56K **bps (bits per second)**. Faster modems can save you money if you are charged by the amount of time you spend on the Web. You will need a computer that has at least 16MB **(megabytes)** of **RAM (random-access memory)**. (*Note:* You will also need to find out the networking capabilities of your ISP; information is transferred only as fast as your ISP's slowest connection.)

For software, you will need **TCP/IP (transmission control protocol/Internet protocol**—languages that allow computers to communicate with each other) to provide an interface between your computer and the Internet. If you have a Macintosh, you need MacTCP. If you have an IBM or clone, you need Winsock (which stands for "Windows socket"). Generally these networking protocol utilities are already provided with your computer system. There are two main types of browsers, graphic and text-only, which are explained in more detail on pages 3 and 4.

Client/Server Systems

The Web works on a client/server system. The **client** is your computer and software; a server is any computer that houses files (text, audio, video, software) you want; and **networks** are systems that connect clients and servers. Think of your computer (the client) as a customer in a restaurant and the information provider (the server) as the chef. You order a meal (the information), and the waiter or waitress (the network) brings it back to you (your computer).

URLs and How They Work

To access a file by means of a Web browser, you must know the file's location. A **URL (uniform resource locator),** the Internet address for a file, is composed as follows:

```
protocol://server and domain name/file path/file
```

For example, suppose a student named Jane Smith at the University of Tennessee, Knoxville, has created a personal Web page for her résumé. The address for that page might be as follows:

```
http://funnelweb.utcc.utk.edu/~jSmith/Resume.html
```

Here, `http` is the **protocol**; `funnelweb.utcc.utk.edu` is the server and **domain name**; `~jSmith` is the **file path**; and `Resume.html` is the file. When you type this address in Netscape or Lynx, the browser reads the URL's components to find the specific page. The first part of the URL not only tells you what type of file you are accessing, but it also tells the computer what kind of language it needs to speak. In this case, you want a Web page in **HTML (hypertext mark-up language),** so the computer needs to speak hypertext, using HTTP (hypertext transfer protocol).

The next thing your computer needs to know is where the file is kept. This is what the second part of the URL, the server and domain name, designates. The server where the Web page in this example is kept is called `funnelweb`. The funnelweb server is a computer at the University of Tennessee, Knoxville (UTK), that is denoted by `utcc.utk.edu.` The `.edu` tells you that the domain is "educational." Other types of domains are `.com` for "commercial"; `.mil` for "military"; `.org` for "organizational"; `.net` for "network"; and `.gov` for "governmental" sites. Recently, seven new domain categories were added: `.firm` for "business"; `.store` for "retail"; .nom for "individual"; .rec for "recreational"; .info for "informational"; .arts for "cultural"; and .web for "Web-oriented" sites. Of all the Web pages at UTK, how does your computer know which one is Jane Smith's? The last two parts of the URL tell how to get to Jane Smith's file. (Note the tilde symbol [~], which is generally used to indicate a personal page.) The user identification for Jane's file path, or "user area," is ~jSmith. The file your computer wants is Resume.html. Now that the computer knows where to go, which file to get, and how to read it, the computer can display Jane Smith's page on your browser's screen (such as Netscape or Lynx). Notice that the file name has a mix of upper- and lowercase letters. Most URLs are case sensitive, so be sure to enter the URL exactly, including the uppercase letters. Note also that URLs never contain spaces.

Downloading Information

When you access a page, it sometimes takes a long time for the page to appear on your screen. If you are using Netscape and look at the bottom of the browser window while waiting for a Web page to appear, you should see a display indicating the percentage of the amount of data transferred. When you access a Web page, a copy of the file is transferred to your computer's memory. This is called **downloading** a file. So, when you are **surfing** the Web, copies of all those Web pages are downloaded to your computer. However, the file is not downloaded all at once; it is transferred in pieces, or **packets.** Depending on the size of the files you are downloading, the length of time it takes for the Web page to appear will vary: A large Web page or a Web page with lots of graphics will slow the transfer. Image files are larger than text files and take longer to download. To shorten the download time in Netscape, turn off Auto Load Images (from the Preferences menu under "View"). Also turn off **Java** loading. To remove the check mark, click on Auto Load Images. To turn Auto Load Images back on, simply click on that line and it will be reactivated. By turning off Images, Web pages containing graphics will download faster, but you will not see any of the graphics automatically. To see the graphics individually, you have to click on each picture frame; to see all the graphics at once, turn Auto Load Images back on and click on Reload (from the View menu) or on the Reload button on the toolbar. Your computer stores Web pages it has loaded in its **cache;** some computers empty their cache automatically, while with others you may need to empty it yourself.

Internet Service Providers

To get onto the Internet, you will need an ISP. Before looking into commercial ISPs, check with your college or university's computing center because some schools offer Internet services for home access to students, faculty, and staff. Internet services through your school will probably be the best deal. Although your school may not always have the latest upgrades of hardware or software, the price will probably be hard to beat.

If you decide to go with a commercial ISP, you should do some comparison shopping. Think about what you will be using your Internet connection for, such as e-mail, Internet mail, graphic access to the Web, file transfer, Telnet, or storing Web pages. Once you decide what you will need, find out which ISPs offer all those services. After you have gathered a list of possible providers, ask some questions:

- What is the level of customer support, such as online help, user manuals, and telephone support (preferably 24 hours)?
- Is there an installation fee?
- Is there an extra cost for e-mail? If so, is the charge by message, by time, or by size of the message? Is there a storage fee for mail?
- Are there different rates for access at different times of the day?
- Is there a local dial-in number? Will long-distance fees be charged?
- What is the **bandwidth** (the amount of information that can be transferred across a network at one time)? The size of the bandwidth can affect access speed.
- Is all the necessary software provided, such as TCP/IP and a browser (such as Netscape or Explorer)?
- Is storage space available for Web pages? If so, what is the charge?
- Are backup servers available to help maintain continuous access?
- What kind of security is offered?
- Read some reviews, such as those from *PC Week* (also available on the Web).

How to Find the Information You Want

The Internet is a vast and rapidly changing conglomeration of information. Finding your way to the particular piece of information you need can be difficult if you are not familiar with the search options available.

World Wide Web Search Engines
You can search the Web with **search engines** such as Yahoo! or AltaVista; search FTP archives with **Archie** and **ArchiePlex;** burrow through **Gopher** with **Veronica,** Archie, **Jughead,** and Gopher Jewels; and access library computers directly with Hytelnet <http://www.lights.com/hytelnet>.

A Note on the URLs in This Book

Change is inherent in the Web. As we prepared this guide, we verified every URL we list. But, by the time you read this book, some of the URLs will almost certainly have changed. If you cannot find one of these URLs, try deleting the last set of letters in the URL (going "up" a level in the address). If that does not work, try searching for the page's title in your favorite search engine, such as Yahoo! or AltaVista.

Sometimes the problem is *not finding enough information;* more often the problem is *finding way too much information;* and, always, the problem is *finding the right information.* Here are some suggestions for solving these problems.

Search engines are computer programs that allow you to find the information you want through key word searches. The search engine provides a text box, into which you type key words associated with the information you want. Most search engines also offer more complex searches involving some variation of **Boolean logic** with the aid of "logical operators," such as AND, OR, and NOT. (Some search engines let "+" stand for AND and "–" stand for NOT.) Some even offer more advanced searching, such as limiting your search to specific dates, ranking key words in order of appearance within the document, or giving you other ways to refine your search.

There are hundreds of search engines for the Internet—too many to discuss here. Two popular and different types of search engines, Yahoo! (a searchable, browsable directory) and AltaVista (a powerful search engine), are briefly described below. For a more extensive list of search engines, see the Library of Congress list at <http://lcweb.loc.gov/global/search.html>.

Yahoo! <http://www.yahoo.com>. Yahoo! is both a search engine and a directory made of subject trees. A **subject tree** is a hierarchical index system for finding information. You begin with a general subject, such as Medicine, and follow the subject tree's branches to a specific document. Yahoo!'s subject trees begin on its main page, which can be found at its URL.

Yahoo! is a good way to start searching because it looks at only a few key elements. Consequently, Yahoo! is the place to go for general discussions of your topic. To learn more about how to do a search on Yahoo!, click on the Options link located by the text box where you type in your key words.

AltaVista <http://www.altavista.com>. Unlike Yahoo!, AltaVista does a thorough full-text search of documents for key words. If you put a fairly general key word into AltaVista, you will most likely receive hundreds or even thousands of links to pages that may only mention your topic in passing. AltaVista is a good place to search for obscure items or for very specific topics.

If you are getting too many hits for a topic on AltaVista, try doing the same search on Yahoo!; this should cut down the number of possible matches. Likewise, if you are searching on Yahoo! and you are not getting enough matches, try AltaVista.

AltaVista offers both a Simple Search and an Advanced Search. The Advanced Search helps you limit your results by specifying date ranges and ranking key words. To find out more about Simple and Advanced Searches on AltaVista, click the Help button at the top of the first AltaVista page.

Metasearch engines. Today there are a number of metasearch engines—search engines that search a number of other search engines at one time. For example, on Dogpile (<http://www.dogpile.com>), instead of getting a result such as "15 hits found," you may read "5 hits on Yahoo!; 10 hits on AltaVista; 12 hits on InfoSeek," etc. Then you can choose which results you may want to look at. This feature is often a great timesaver. Interestingly, however, the same search that may turn up 15 hits on AltaVista if you use a metasearch engine, may turn up 25 hits if you search on AltaVista alone. As a consequence, while some people prefer metasearch engines, others (including this book's authors) prefer to use one or two or three separate search engines consistently. (Other metasearch engines are listed at <http://www.islandnet.com/~pb/frames.html>.)

Searching via Key Words

Key word searches may require some imagination if you are not getting the results you hoped for. In most cases, your search was either too narrow or too broad. The tips below should help. Also, when you do find information you want, remember to check it for credibility. (See pages 16–18 on how to judge the reliability of Internet information.)

Narrowing a search. If you are getting too many **hits** (successful key word matches), try narrowing your search by adding more key words. Sometimes this will help, because most search engines will look for each of the words independently but display the pages with the most matches first. Usually, you can narrow your search and make sure that all the key words appear in the document by using AND between the key words.

⌐🖰 **Info Bit**—Narrow your search by looking for the most current information (or for the most relevant dates) in the AltaVista Advanced Search by entering a starting and an ending date for the information.

⤒ *Info Bit*—Some search engines, such as Yahoo!, allow you to search within document titles only. This will narrow your search results and may give you better sources on your topic.

Broadening a search. If you are not getting enough hits, you need to broaden your search by deleting some of the more specific key words or substituting synonyms for the key words you already have listed. For example, for a search about how to make a Web page, you might try several search strings, such as "Web page design," "creating a Web page," and "making a Web page." Also, you may want to try a more general category under which your topic falls. For example, if you want information on the Hopi god Kokopeli, but you get only one or two hits, you could try searching for "Hopi religion" or just "Hopi."

⤒ *Info Bit*—The Web is a big place with millions of documents, and it is growing by the hour. No single search engine can cover the whole Web. Each search engine covers different, although overlapping, territory. If your search does not work with the first engine you use, try running it on several different ones, or try a metasearch engine.

⤒ *Info Bit*—Some search engines are designed to find specific topics, such as Law Crawler at <http://www.lawcrawler.com> or the Amazing Environmental Organization Web Directory at <http://www. webdirectory.com>.

Finding phrases. If you want to find documents containing a specific phrase, such as "Green Bay Packers," put the phrase in double quotation marks to lock them together. Otherwise you will get thousands of pages that have only "green" or "bay" or "packers" in them.

Searching via Subject Trees
As described previously in the section on Yahoo!, a subject tree is a hierarchical index of topics that allows you to begin with a broad category and follow the subject tree's branches down to a specific file. Subject trees can be good places to start your search because you can get an idea of the different types of information available on your topic.

One of the first and best subject trees is The Virtual Library <http:// www.w3.org/vl>. There are different ways to search The Virtual Library. You can start searching the Subject Index on the main page, or you can search the Category Subtree or the Top Ten Most Popular Fields.

Other Places to Start
You can start your Web research in many places besides search engines. One possibility is traditional reference tools (such as encyclopedias) that

Info Byte: Some Common Error Messages

Connection refused by server

Server is busy. The maximum number of simultaneous connections has probably been reached. Try again later.

Document contains no data

First, try clicking the link again. If this doesn't work, there may be a glitch in the network.

Forbidden access (Error 401)

For some reason, the creator or maintainer of a page does not want any "outside" visitors, and he or she has restricted the access to the page.

No DNS entry

Means "No Domain Name System," or that the server does not exist. If you are linking to a page from another, try clicking the link again. If you are entering the URL, make sure you have entered it correctly—with any capital letters and without spaces. If the URL is correct, the server may not be working.

Not found (Error 404)

The file you are looking for is not on this server. It may have been moved or deleted.

No response

There may be too many connections, or the server may be down for some reason. Try again later.

Transfer interrupted!

For some reason, the server was not able to transfer all of the data for this page. Try reloading.

Error 400

Your request could not be understood by the server. Your Web browser may be malfunctioning or your Internet connection may be unreliable. Try shutting down and restarting your computer.

are increasingly available on the Web. For example, *Encyclopaedia Britannica* is now available online, free, at <http://www.britannica.com>. Many teachers believe the best way to begin a research project is to consult such traditional reference tools; more and more of these are available on the Web.

Another possible place to start your Web research is to think about what kind of place might be likely to have information on your subject, and look for that place's Web site. For example, if you're researching a medical topic, why not start at the National Institutes of Health's home page (<http://www. nih.gov/>)? If you're writing about the FBI, remember to look at the FBI's own site (<http://www.fbi.gov/>). If you're writing about any kind of historical topic, from the Dead Sea Scrolls to the Civil War, why not start at the Smithsonian (<http://www.si.edu/>)? Giving a few minutes' thought to what kind of place would be likely to have good information on your topic, and to finding and checking that place's Web site, can pay big dividends in research success. You can also try library search engines, especially the Library of Congress (<http://www.lcweb.loc.gov/>). (Be aware that library search engines often operate under a tighter set of search rules than Internet search engines, so if the key word you have chosen to use on a library search engine is not retrieving the kinds of sources you are looking for, you may need to try other key words or get help from a librarian.)

Other Protocols: Telnet and Gopher
Web servers communicate through HTTP (hypertext transfer protocol), but there are other, older information systems, such as Telnet and Gopher, that communicate through other protocols. The URLs for these other Internet systems begin with a different protocol abbreviation, or prompt, such as `telnet://`, `gopher://`, or `ftp://`. Telnet and Gopher are described here; FTP (file transfer protocol) is discussed in Chapter Three.

Telnet. Some electronic **bulletin boards,** library catalogs, and school computer accounts are not part of the Web. To access these sources, you can use **Telnet,** a protocol that lets you communicate with computers that use the UNIX operating system. To use Telnet, you need to log on to another computer (a remote host). When you log on, a text-only screen identical to the screen of the remote host will appear. Then you can issue commands from your computer and have them carried out by the remote host.

A Telnet session's first screen usually lists instructions for logging on, accessing the Help page, and logging off. If you get a blank screen, try pressing Enter (or Return). If you get a screen with instructions, *read it carefully,* because when you want to exit a session, you may not remember how. If no instructions are given, try typing ? and pressing Enter to get the

Help page. To exit, hold the Command key and type q if you are using a Macintosh, or hold the Control key and type q if you are using a PC.

To use Telnet, you will need Telnet software. If your ISP does not provide the software, you can download it from the Internet for free. For a Macintosh, get Better Telnet at <http://www.cstone.net/~rbraun/mac/telnet/>. For a PC, get EWAN Telnet from <http://www.iconn.iphil.net/services/telnet.html>.

Gopher. Gopher is a menu-driven information system started at the University of Minnesota and named after its mascot, the "Gophers." It is a predecessor of the World Wide Web. However, Gopher menu systems and files can be accessed via the Web. There is a lot of good information on Gopher that is not available elswhere on the Internet. If you want to search Gopher, a good place to start is with Gopher Jewels at <http://www.uccs.edu/gopher/jewels.html>. Gopher Jewels catalogs many Gopher sites by subject tree. For a more thorough search of Gopher sites, use a search engine, such as Jughead (document title search) or Veronica (full-text search). For more on Gopher, Veronica, and Jughead, go to <http://lcweb.loc.gov/loc/guides/navigate.html>.

Integrating Research Sources

While the focus of this book is the World Wide Web, with particular attention to doing research on the Web and correctly citing your Web sources in your research papers, it needs to be pointed out that few college teachers today will accept papers that use *only* Web-based research, and some teachers frown on using *any* Web-based research. Thus, even if you are in a situation where Web research is acceptable, chances are you will need to integrate your Web research with information from traditional print sources as well. Here are two ways to go about integrating your research sources, accompanied by "road maps" to help you visualize each process.

Past-Present-Future (or General to Specific). A traditional approach to library research would suggest starting with reference tools (such as encyclopedias), moving on to books (by way of the *Library of Congress Subject Headings* list), and then going to periodical publications (via periodical indexes). Finally, with a wealth of background information in hand, you could go on to collect firsthand information—from interviews, direct observation, surveys, laboratory tests, or fieldwork. Within this structure, shown in Road Map One, the *last* step would be to do Web-based research, perhaps using as search terms in Yahoo! and AltaVista the key words (including author's names) gathered from all the earlier research steps. This

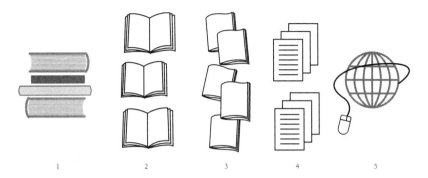

Road Map One: 1 = *reference tools;* 2 = *books;* 3 = *periodical articles;*
4 = *primary research;* 5 = *Web-based research*

method starts slowly but hardly ever fails to produce rich results. The
downside is that it starts so slowly and the early stages are not much fun;
consequently, some students tend to put off starting until it really is too
late for this rather deliberate process to work. The upside is that given
enough time and effort, the process just about always works.

Start Hot, Finish Strong. Few people who become accustomed to
doing research on the Web can resist the temptation to at least try their
topic in a few search engines before they do anything else. Suppose you
are writing about "the role of sign language interpreters in the CIA"—
why not try that phrase, and a few variations of it, in your favorite search
engines before you do anything else? If you get some good hits, you can
still proceed backward through the previous pattern (roughly, Web materials, then print periodical articles, then books, then reference tools, then
firsthand research), working from leads in Web-based sources (authors'
names, possible bibliographical information) through increasingly broader
(and, usually, older) sources. This method is shown in Road Map Two.

Two cautions go with this method: First, if you do not find good Web
sources in the first step, you probably need to use the Past-Present-Future
method instead. Second, no matter how good the Web sources you may find
in the first step are, you *must still* do the other steps, and do them carefully
and thoroughly. Otherwise, you will risk writing a paper that is shallow and
one-dimensional, and, because you are relying too much on few sources of
only one kind, the possibility of accidental plagiarism is strong. The weak

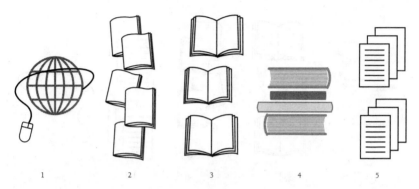

Road Map Two: *1 = Web-based research; 2 = periodical articles; 3 = books; 4 = reference sources; 5 = primary research*

side of this process is that some students are tempted to stop after the first step. The strong side is that if you do get some good hits early on, that rush of initial success can carry you forward pretty far into the process.

How to Judge the Reliability of Internet Information

Students who are accustomed to doing research in libraries face new issues when they start doing research on the Internet. Before a book or journal appears in a university library, it has usually gone through a number of checks to make sure the information in it is reliable. For example, if you find a copy of *Moby Dick* in your university library, you can be sure you are getting a generally accepted version of the real thing. But if you find a copy of *Moby Dick* on the Internet, you need to give some thought to *where you found it,* whether the person who put it on the Internet is *a reliable authority on the subject* (someone who can be trusted not to enter his or her own personal, political, or scholarly biases into the text), and whether your professor will *accept your judgment* of the reliability of that material.

Arguably, student researchers should always make these decisions, even about materials they find in the university library. However, judging the reliability of sources found on the Internet is crucial because there is no regulating body that monitors the reliability of what is on the Internet. Although there is so much information on the Internet that it can seem like a university library, it is actually more like a huge open-air market. In one corner there might be reliable sources from whom you can obtain valuable information. But over in another corner there might be weirdos, whackos, and eccentrics, from whom anything you obtain is, at best, questionable. The problem is that on the Internet there is no way to tell the difference. Someone who wants to turn *Moby Dick* into a glorification of bloodsports or an animal rights tract can post a rewritten version with no indication of its differences from Melville's original. There's a saying in Latin, *caveat emptor,* or "let the buyer beware." When it comes to doing your research on the Internet, the saying should be *caveat internauta,* or "let the surfer beware."

Here is a list of points to consider when you are trying to judge the reliability of information you find on the Internet:

- **Who is the author or sponsor of the page?** On the page you are citing, or on a page linked to it, that individual or organization should be identified, that individual's qualifications should be apparent, and other avenues of verification should be open to you. For a good example of a reliable source, see "Notes about this document" for the hypertext version of *Pride and Prejudice* at <http://www.pemberley.com/janeinfo/pridprej.html>. A page created by a person or an organization that does not provide this information is *not* a good source to cite. (You can often find out more about a page's source by deleting the last section of its URL and Reloading your browser, thus moving up a level in the Web site's hierarchy.)

- **Are there obvious reasons for bias?** If the page is presented by a tobacco company consortium, you should be suspicious of its reports on the addictiveness of nicotine. Is there any advertising? If the page is sponsored by Acme Track Shoes, you should be suspicious of its claims for Acme track shoes' performance.

- **Is contact information provided?** If the only identification available is something cryptic, such as "Society for Feruginous Retorts," be suspicious of the page's reliability. If the page is sponsored by a reputable person or organization, there should be some other way to verify that reputation, such as an e-mail or a postal address. (Note that a tilde [~] in the page's address usually indicates a personal home page and may require more searching for reliability.)

- **Is there a copyright symbol on the page?** If so, who holds the copyright?

- **Is this page a "zombie,"** or one considered "walking dead" because the person who posted it no longer maintains or updates it? Even though the information is "alive" in that it is still accessible, it is "dead" in that it may no longer be accurate. Look for a last-updated date if your topic requires current information.

- **What is the purpose of the page?** Why is this information being posted—as information, as a public service, as news, as a research tool for academics, as a personal ax to grind, or as a way to gain attention?

- **How well organized is the page?** Is the page easy to navigate? Is it complete? How credible are the links it provides?

- **Is the information on the page *primary* or *secondary*?** That is, is it a report of facts, such as a medical researcher's article counting cases of "mad cow" disease in England, thus making it primary information, or is it an Internet newsgroup discussion about "mad cow" disease, thus making it secondary information? The papers and reports you write for your college classes need to be based on primary information whenever possible. The further away from the primary sources your own sources are, the less reliable the information may be.

- **Can you verify the information** on the Web page some other way? For example, can you check the page's bibliography (if there is one) against your library's holdings or check the information against a source in the library?

- **If you are worried that the information may lack credibility, try starting with a source you know is reputable.** For example, if you have to do a project on the latest in cancer research, you can begin your search at major cancer research institutes, such as the Mayo Clinic in Rochester, Minnesota <http://www.mayo.edu>.

- Finally, remember that **even though a page might not meet your standards as a citable source, it may provide good ideas** or point to other usable sources. Also, be sure not to stop your search at the first page you find—shop around and do some comparing so that you can have points of reference.

Ultimately, the problem with reliability of information on the Web is like the whispering game children play. Someone whispers a message to the first child, who whispers it to the second, and so on. By the time it gets to the last child, the message is hopelessly distorted. Web pages can work the same way when people get their information from other people's Web pages: The first person who posts information may make a few small errors, the second unintentionally repeats them and makes one or two more, the third makes a few more, and so on. For information seekers it can be impossible to tell where in the chain the information is coming from, but that makes a difference in the information's reliability. So it is always a good idea to check against a library reference.

CHAPTER TWO
HOW TO DOCUMENT INFORMATION
FROM ELECTRONIC SOURCES

Whenever you are doing research and writing for a classroom assignment, documenting your sources correctly is important. If the information, ideas, or other kinds of materials (such as drawings and graphics) in your paper are from a source, you need to let your readers know by adding appropriate documentation. (And if you quote passages, you need to add quotation marks or make block quotations as well.) The documentation you provide needs to be complete enough that a reader who wants to check your sources will be able to find them. Material borrowed from the Internet and other electronic sources, just like print sources, must be properly documented. This chart compares the elements of documentation for print sources with those of documentation for electronic sources.

Books	Articles	Electronic Sources
Full name of author or editor	Full name of author	Full name of author (if available)
Exact title	Exact title	Exact title
Place of publication and publisher	Journal name	Type of source (Web page, FTP site, online journal, CD-ROM, etc.)
	Volume and issue (if pages are numbered consecutively throughout the volume, you can omit issue number)	
Year of publication	Year of publication	Date accessed
Page numbers	Page numbers	URL (if appropriate)

Portable versus Online Sources

There are two kinds of electronic sources of information—*unchangeable* and *changeable*—and they need to be documented in slightly different ways.

Portable (or Unchangeable) Sources
Suppose you look up material on a **CD-ROM (compact disc, read-only memory)**, such as InfoTrac, Encarta, or some other portable database. As an electronic source, the CD-ROM is stable—that is, anyone could look at it today, next month, or next year, and find the same information. It has a date and place of publication (although here "publication" actually means "production") and a version number, which should be shown in your documentation just as they would be for a journal article. Thus, for unchangeable sources there is no need to add extra elements to your documentation.

Online (or Changeable) Sources
For materials you find on the Internet, you need to add some information to your documentation. Usually, it includes the date you accessed the information and its URL. Sometimes, you may be required to include the path you took to get to the page or even a hard copy (a printout) of the page. If information you find on the Internet is crucial to your work, it is always a good idea to print out a hard copy, just in case.

Different Styles for Different Fields

If you are taking a sociology class, your teacher may require you to use the American Psychological Association (APA) style, which is also what academics in the social sciences, such as psychology or education, generally use. English or composition classes use Modern Language Association (MLA) style, which is what literature and language specialists use. When documenting Web and Internet sources, many teachers of first-year students recommend the Alliance for Computers and Writing (ACW) style <http://english.ttu.edu/acw>. Professors for higher-level classes or classes in other fields may expect you to use some other style—the Council of Biology Editors (CBE) style used in the life sciences; the *Chicago Manual of Style* (CMS) superscript style used in business, history, and many hard sciences; or even the Institute of Electrical and Electronics Engineers (IEEE) style <http://www.ieee.org> used in fields such as computer science. Although there are hundreds of different styles, the right one for you will probably look close to one of the four varieties presented here.

When and What to Document

Here are seven simple guidelines to help you decide when and what to document:

1. If you use the exact language of your source, you must use quotation marks, or set the quote off as a block, and cite the source.

2. If you put the source's information into your own words (creating a paraphrase), you *still* must cite your source.

3. Use direct quotations only if there is something unique about your source's language or if your own words will not do the job better.

4. Directly quote only as much as you need—the bare minimum.

5. If you use information that is not common knowledge, you must cite the source. If this information would not be familiar to someone who had not researched the subject, it is not common knowledge and its source must be cited.

6. Cite all kinds of sources, not just words and facts. Sources can also include drawings, photos, artwork, ideas, music—anything you use that is not yours.

7. To work your quoted or otherwise borrowed material into the text more smoothly, introduce it with the name of the source. To introduce your borrowed material, use a tag line—for example, "As Dr. Stanley Prusiner, one of the leading authorities on prion diseases, said. . . ."

QUICK VIEW
AMERICAN PSYCHOLOGICAL ASSOCIATION (APA)
AUTHOR-DATE STYLE

APA style places the author's name and date of publication within parentheses in the text, linked to a list of references (titled *References*) at the end of the document. Although the focus of this guide is electronic sources, here is a brief overview of APA documentation style. For more information, consult the *Publication Manual of the American Psychological Association,* 4th edition (1994).

Citations in the Text

Citations in the text generally include the author's last name and the year in parentheses. So a citation to something by Bill Jones in 1988 would be (Jones, 1988). The parenthetical citation precedes the sentence's final punctuation. If the author's name has already appeared in the sentence, the year of publication follows it in parentheses. APA requires page numbers only if you are citing a direct quotation or a specific table, figure, or equation. If you need to include page numbers (and some teachers want page numbers for everything), use *p.* or *pp.*

Parenthetical citations for direct quotations in the text appear after the closing quotation marks but before the final punctuation. If the quotation is more than forty words long, it should be indented an inch. If the quotation is set off, the citation appears after the quotation's final punctuation.

Entries in the References List

Each entry in the reference list must match a citation, and the entire list must be double spaced. The entries should be alphabetized by the author's last name and, in the case of multiple entries by the same authors, chronologically, beginning with the earliest. APA recommends that the first line of every entry should be indented and subsequent lines be flush left. Each entry has four elements: author, date, title, and publication information. A typical entry for a book looks like this:

Schultz, E., & Lavenda, R. (1998) <u>Cultural
anthropology: Perspectives on the human condition</u>
(2nd ed.). Mountain View, CA: Mayfield.

Note: We show APA references here with paragraph-style indents; some teachers may prefer "hanging" indents (first line flush left, subsequent lines indented). According to the FAQ on the APA Web site, either style may be acceptable.

APA Style for Citing Electronic Sources

The basic citation has five elements: author, date, title, document type, and publication information. The information here has been supplemented by APA's Web page, "Electronic Reference Formats Recommended by the American Psychological Association" <http://www.apa.org/journals/webref.html>.

CD-ROMs and Other Portable Databases

If you use information from a CD-ROM or other unchangeable source (such as a magnetic tape or commercially produced disk), you need to name the author, date, and title just as for a print source. Next, specify the date accessed and the nature of the electronic medium. At the end of the entry, give the name and source location of the producer. A typical entry looks like this (because there is no author in this example, the publication's name comes first):

> The world factbook 1994. (1994). Washington, DC: Central Intelligence Agency. Retrieved Oct. 10, 1996, from CD-ROM.

You may encounter a CD-ROM version of a document that is also available in hard copy. If so, your citation needs to include information for both (while making it clear that you accessed the CD-ROM version). This note is for an abstract that was read on CD-ROM:

> Morring, F., Jr. (1994, May 16). Russian hardware allows earlier station experiments [Abstract]. Aviation Week & Space Technology, 140, 57. Retrieved Oct. 10, 1996 from CD-ROM: InfoTrac General Periodicals Index-A: Abstract 15482317.

Online Sources

For changeable sources, use this format: author's name, date of the most recent revision (if available), title of the source, date of access, and identification of the type of document (such as online serial or personal home page). In place of a publisher is the complete URL. If the URL will not fit on one line, break it after a period or slash. Here is an example:

> Land, T. (1996, March 31). Web extension to American Psychological Association style (WEAPAS) [online] (Rev. 1.2.4). URL retrieved April 24, 1997 from the World Wide Web: http://www.beadslands.com/weapas/.

QUICK VIEW
Council of Biology Editors (CBE)
Citation-Sequence System

The CBE style manual presents two systems of documentation. The one summarized here uses numbers in the text that refer to a numbered list of references at the end of the document. Because our purpose here is to show how CBE treats electronic sources, we summarize only the citation sequence system. For full details, refer to *Scientific Style and Format: The CBE Manual for Authors, Editors, and Publishers,* 6th edition (1994).

Citations in the Text
When a source is first used in the text, it is assigned a number that it retains whenever it is used again. The number appears in superscript immediately after the source is referred to, not separated by a space. If more than one source is cited, the numbers are separated by commas without spaces. Here is a typical entry (taken from Leslie C. Perelman, James Paradis, and Edward Barrett, *The Mayfield Handbook of Technical and Scientific Writing,* 1998):

> The oncogene jun has presently become one of the best-known oncogenes because of its ability to act as a transcription factor[1]. One study[2] examined
> . . . .

Entries in the References List
Titled *References* or *Cited References,* the whole list is double spaced. The sequence is established by the order in which the items appear in the text. The number of the entry is flush left and is followed by a period. Each entry has four basic elements: author, title, publication information, and page numbers. Authors' first and middle names are abbreviated, as are other elements; the abbreviations are not followed by periods. Here is an example of a journal article entry:

> 1. Lenski RE, May RM. The evolution of virulence in parasites and pathogens: reconciliation between two competing hypotheses. J Theoret Biol 1994;169:253-65.

Here is a typical entry for a book:

> 13. Mandelbrot BB. The fractal geometry of

nature.

San Francisco: WH Freeman; 1995. 460 p.

CBE Style for Citing Electronic Sources

The CBE style for citing electronic sources is still evolving. The pattern for online sources recommended here is taken from *The Mayfield Handbook of Technical and Scientific Writing,* and is consistent with other CBE formats.

CD-ROMs and Other Portable Databases

For unchangeable sources, the author, date, and title information is provided just as for a print source. In brackets after the title, identify the medium. At the end of the entry, include the name of the database and its location. Here is a typical entry:

9. Morring F Jr. Russian hardware allows earlier station experiments [CD-ROM]. Aviat Wk Space Technol 1994;140:57. Abstract from: InfoTrac General Periodicals Index-A: Abstract 15482317.

Online Sources

The *CBE Manual* does not require the full Internet address for changeable sources. Nonetheless, it makes sense to include this additional information. Here is a sample entry with the type of document provided and the URL and date of access added:

1. Brooker MIH, Slee AV. New taxa and some new nomenclature in *Eucalyptus.* Muelleria [abstract online] 1996; 9(75-85). Available from WWW; <http://155.187.10.12/cpbrpublications/ brooker-slee2.html> (Accessed 1997 Feb 13).

QUICK VIEW
CHICAGO MANUAL OF STYLE (CMS) SUPERSCRIPT SYSTEM

Three documentation systems are presented in *The Chicago Manual of Style*, 14th edition (1993). The one shown here uses superscript numbers keyed to numbered endnotes or footnotes. It is based on an adaptation of CMS style for college writers: *A Manual for Writers of Term Papers, Theses, and Dissertations*, 6th edition (1996), by Kate Turabian. In the FAQ on their Web page, the editors of *Chicago* recommend Turabian for writers whose manuscripts will *not* be published as books.

Citations in the Text
Note numbers that appear in the text are superscript numbers. They normally go at the end of the sentence, following the final punctuation; if they must be used within a sentence, they should go after a punctuation mark. CMS superscript notations in the text will look like this:

> One literary critic notes "Austen's uncertainty about the inner life of Darcy,"[1] and another explains that Austen's novels, like those of many other nineteenth-century British authors, empower their heroines "over their own plot" and place them at the center of the action.[2]

If you use a direct quotation in the text, the note number appears after the closing quotation mark. A direct quotation that is eight lines or more should be set off, single spaced, and indented four spaces. The note number appears right after the quotation's final punctuation.

Entries in the Notes List
Each entry in the list of notes should correspond to a superscript number in the text. The entries are arranged numerically, with the reference number followed by a period and a space. The entire list of notes should be double spaced, with the first line of each entry indented half an inch.

Each entry generally has four elements: author, title, publication information, and page numbers. The author's name is given in normal order (first name, then last name). Here is a basic entry for a book:

> 2. Hilary M. Lips, <u>Sex and Gender: An Introduction,</u> 3rd ed. (Mountain View, CA: Mayfield Publishing, 1997), 151.

If note number 3 were to that same source, just a different page, the entry would read

        3. Ibid., 159.

CMS Style for Citing Electronic Sources

The CMS style for citing electronic sources is still evolving. The pattern for unchangeable sources presented here comes from the current (14th) edition. The pattern for changeable sources comes from the adaptation of CMS style by Kate Turabian (cited on the previous page). An excellent online source for more information about adapting CMS style for online documents is the CMS FAQ available at <http://www. press.uchicago.edu/ Misc/Chicago/cmosfaq.html>.

CD-ROMS and Other Portable Databases

For unchangeable electronic sources, the citation is like that for print sources, with the addition of the name of the producer or vendor and any access numbers associated with the document. Here is a sample entry:

        1. Frank Morring, Jr., "Russian Hardware
   Allows Earlier Station Experiments," Aviation Week
   & Space Technology, 16 May 1994, 57; Abstract
   15482317: InfoTrac General Periodicals Index-A
   [CD-ROM], September 1996.

Online Sources

For changeable sources, the entry contains the usual elements for print sources, followed by an indication in square brackets of what type of document it is, the complete document address, and the date of access.

        2. Charles Shepherdson, "History and the
   Real: Foucault with Lacan," Postmodern Culture 5,
   no. 2 (January 1995) [serial online]; available
   from http://jefferson.village.virginia.edu/pmc/
   shepherd.195.html; Internet; accessed 15 May 1995.

QUICK VIEW
MODERN LANGUAGE ASSOCIATION (MLA) AUTHOR-PAGE STYLE

MLA style uses parenthetical citations within the text. They lead readers to
a list of entries at the end of the document called *Works Cited*. Generally,
the material within the parenthetical citation includes the author's name
and the page number to which you are referring. Here we summarize
briefly the MLA style of documentation, and on the next page we go into
more detail about the MLA style for citing electronic sources. If you want
more details about MLA documentation style, consult the *MLA Handbook
for Writers of Research Papers*, 5th edition (1999). A basic MLA citation in
the text will look like this:

```
...leads to better research (Morring 57).
```

This citation would lead readers to the following entry at the end of the
document:

```
Morring, Frank, Jr. "Russian Hardware Allows
Earlier Space Station Experiments." Aviation Week
and Space Technology 16 (May 1994): 57.
```

Citations in the Text
In MLA style, parenthetical citations go at the end of the sentence in which
the source material appears. If the sentence already includes the author's
name, then only the page number appears in the parenthetical citation. In
the case of more than one work by the same author, a short title is added
in the parentheses. The page number is given in the parentheses, without
p. or *pp.*

Parenthetical citations for direct quotations in the text appear after the
closing quotation mark but before the final punctuation. Direct quotations
that are more than four lines long should be indented an inch rather than
enclosed in quotation marks. The parenthetical reference for such quotations follows the quotation's final punctuation.

Entries in the Works Cited List
The list of works cited includes only sources mentioned in the text and not
all sources consulted. Entries are arranged alphabetically by the author's
last name (or by the first significant word in the title if there is no author).
The page is double spaced, with the first line of each entry flush left and
subsequent lines indented half an inch (or five spaces on a typewriter).
The basic pattern of an entry is author's name, title, and publication information (place, name of publisher, date, and page numbers).

MLA Style for Citing Electronic Sources

The MLA style for citing electronic sources is still evolving. Presented here is information from the current *MLA Handbook* (1999) as supplemented by MLA's Web site <http://www.mla.org/style/sources.htm>.

CD-ROMs and Other Portable Databases

For unchangeable sources, the citation in the *Works Cited* list includes the author, title, and date information just as for print documents. After the title of the database, there is a period, followed by the producer's name and date of the product, if available. Finally, include the date you accessed the information.

> Morring, Frank, Jr. "Russian Hardware Allows Earlier Space Station Experiments." <u>Aviation Week and Space Technology</u> 16 (May 1994): 57. <u>InfoTrac: General Periodicals Index</u>. 10 Oct. 1998.

Online Sources

For changeable sources, use this format: author's name, full title (articles in quotation marks, books underlined) and any larger document of which it is a part, date of publication or most recent revision, date accessed, and the full URL address enclosed in angle brackets (< >). Here are two examples:

> Shepherdson, Charles. "History and the Real: Foucault with Lacan." <u>Postmodern Culture</u> 5.2 (Jan. 1995). 15 May 1995 <http://jefferson.village.virginia. edu/pmc/shepherd.195.html>.

> Harnack, Andrew, and Gene Kleppinger. "Beyond the MLA Handbook: Documenting Electronic Sources on the Internet." <u>Kairos</u> 1.2 (1996). 10 Oct. 1996 <http://english.ttu.edu/kairos/1.2>.

Ideally, the URL should not be interrupted by a line break; however, if it is too long to fit on one line, break the URL after a period or slash. The same form is used for a document retrieved from a file transfer protocol (FTP) archive, except the abbreviation ftp precedes the address, and the URL is not enclosed in angle brackets.

CHAPTER THREE
COMMUNICATING ON THE INTERNET

Chapter One of this guide explained some of the most important ways people use the Internet to find information. The subject of this chapter is how to use the Internet to communicate with other people. Of course, making a distinction between these two activities is misleading. For example, when you join an e-mail listserv on the subject of technical communication <listserv@listserv.okstate.edu> because you want to learn more about the field and maybe find an internship, your primary motive may be communication, but you are certainly also finding information.

Communicating on the Internet takes many forms. Here is an overview of the topics discussed in this section:

- E-mail—How to send e-mail to your friends all over the world, how to read e-mail addresses, and how to use Internet mail.

- Netiquette—What you should and shouldn't do when you are communicating on the Internet.

- Discussion groups—How to subscribe to listserv mailing lists (and how to unsubscribe), how to take part in Usenet newsgroups.

- Real-time communication—What is Internet Relay Chat (IRC); what are MOOs, MUDs, MUSHs, and WOOs; what is videoconferencing?

- Electronic file transfer—An introduction to File Transfer Protocol (FTP) and how to do it.

- Risks and precautions—Find out what you need to know about computer security, disclosing personal information, copyright, libel, plagiarism, and viruses.

How to Communicate with E-Mail

E-mail is a way of sending messages electronically. If you get e-mail service through an ISP, you will be given a mailbox and software for reading and storing your mail, for composing and sending messages, and for creating mailing lists. There are lots of different e-mail software packages available, but they all work in much the same way. Most Web browsers such as Netscape and Explorer have built-in e-mail software.

When someone sends you a message, it will be temporarily stored on your ISP's mail server. You will use your e-mail software to see if you have any messages waiting. If you do, the e-mail software will download them from the mail server to your computer, where you can read, store, delete, reply to, print, or forward them.

When you get an e-mail account, you will be given an e-mail address. The address has three parts: for example, user_name@domain_name. Usually, you will be able to create your own user name, which is how your mailbox is identified. The "at" sign (@) separates the user name from the domain name. The domain name is the name of the computer or system where your e-mail is stored.

In the above e-mail address, "user_name" and "domain_name" have no spaces (which is indicated by the underscore)—e-mail addresses cannot have any spaces. The address is also in all lowercase, because e-mail addresses are not case sensitive and are easier to read and type without caps. If you get mail returned because the address could not be found, make sure you have entered it correctly. If you have, and the mail is still returned, the person may have changed addresses or may be having problems with the mail system.

Internet Mail
Internet mail (e-mail sent over the Internet) takes e-mail a step further. For example, suppose you are surfing the Web and find a page that has great information, and you want to get in touch with the person who created the page. Usually, the person who created the page will include a link for sending e-mail. When you click the link, a window will appear where you can type and send a message. However, you need **SMTP (simple mail transfer protocol)** to send the message. Check with your ISP for the name of its SMTP server. To receive Internet e-mail, you will also need a **POP (post office protocol)** server. Check with your ISP for a list of services to see if POP mail accounts are available.

Virtual Communities: Listservs and Newsgroups

Virtual communities are ways of organizing or connecting people of like interests over the Internet. The following section discusses some modes of communication that are analogous to print newsletters.

Listserv Mailing Lists
Listservs are servers that house **mailing lists.** Listserv mailing lists are discussion groups categorized by special interest. Unlike Usenet newsgroups, which let you browse messages posted on Usenet (discussed next), listserv mail messages are sent directly to your e-mail address. When a member posts a message to the listserv, the message is delivered to every subscriber.

When you subscribe, your name and e-mail address are added to the mailing list. From that point on, you will receive all e-mail messages that

---

🖱 *Info Byte: Netiquette*

As with all human communities, even virtual ones, there is acceptable and unacceptable behavior. **Netiquette,** the guidelines for communicating with others on the Internet, helps us all respect the people who share our cyberspace. Most netiquette guidelines are just common sense, a reminder that even though we're in cyberspace, our relations with others are still human relations. Here are some tips:

- Do not use foul or abusive language.

- Do not force offensive material on unwilling participants.

- Do not join in **flaming** (by sending cruel e-mail to someone). Usually, flaming is started over not-so-commonsense breaches of netiquette.

- Do not shout (that is, do not use all caps) at other people on the Internet.

- Do not take off on tangents that are too far from a discussion group's stated purpose.

- Do not post ambiguous questions or ask questions that are answered in a group's Frequently Asked Questions (FAQ) list.

- Be careful to avoid **spamming,** or sending the same message (like a sales pitch) to many different addresses, especially listservs. Spamming is the equivalent of junk mail and will get you flamed in no time.

- Reread your Internet messages before sending them. Something written in haste may be misread.

- Lurk before you leap. (People who subscribe to a listserv and read its messages but do not post any of their own are said to be lurking.) Lurk for a couple of weeks and give yourself a chance to learn that virtual community's rules and temperament before you start posting. This precaution can protect you from making **newbie** mistakes and possibly getting flamed as a result.

---

are posted to the group. It is always wise to **lurk** (hang out and just read messages) for a while before joining the discussion. When you reply to an e-mail message from a listserv, you can mail the person who sent the message originally or you can post your response to the entire group.

One way to find a listserv for people with a particular interest is to do a key word search on a search engine, such as Yahoo! or AltaVista, by entering the topic and the word listserv. Or you can use the extensive mailing lists categorized by subject at "Liszt, the Mailing List Directory" <http://www.liszt.com>.

To subscribe to a list, send an e-mail message to the listserv address. Do not put anything in the subject line of the message. Then, on the first line of the body of the message, type the following:

SUB listname your full name

Once you subscribe, you will receive a set of instructions for list members. It will tell you where to post messages (usually a different address than the subscription address) and what subscription options you have (such as "digest," which combines each day's postings into one packet, or "unsubscribe"). Be sure to save this message!

To unsubscribe, send an e-mail message to the listserv subscription address. Again, do not put anything in the subject line of the message. Then, on the first line of the body of the message, type the following:

UNSUB listname your full name

Remember to unsubscribe if you terminate your e-mail account. Only you can unsubscribe your name from a list.

Usenet Newsgroups

Usenet is a computer network accessible on the Internet that is mainly used for discussion groups. **Newsgroups** are discussion groups on Usenet organized by interest categories. Newsgroups are essentially sets of archived messages, articles, or postings. You are free to browse any newsgroup's articles.

To access newsgroups, you need a newsreader. Most graphic browsers, such as Netscape and Explorer, come equipped with a newsreader. The next thing you need to know is the Network News Transfer Protocol (NNTP) server. Contact your ISP to find out the name of its NNTP server. Once you find out your NNTP server, you will need to adjust your Preferences setup. You will usually be given the choice to edit Mail and News Preferences, and you will find a space to add the name of the NNTP server. When you have finished, save your changes. You may have to restart your browser for the change to take effect. Now you can use the browser's newsreader to browse and respond to newsgroup discussions.

Newsgroups have many **threads** of discussion. A thread is the original message that begins a discussion and all of the replies to that message. Most browsers have options for following threads. For example, when you pull up a newsgroup article in Netscape, there are links at the top of the article to all of the messages in that thread.

Newsgroup articles can literally be here today and gone tomorrow. Because of the thousands of articles a newsgroup can receive in a day, old articles are deleted to make room for the new ones. Depending on how busy a newsgroup is, articles may be deleted within several hours. If you find an article you may want to refer to later, save or print a copy, because it may not be there the next time you look. To save a document as a file on your computer's hard drive, select Save from the File menu and choose a destination.

When accessing newsgroups, some of your basic options are to browse, read, or save newsgroup messages; to reply only to the person who posted a message or to the entire newsgroup; or to post a new message that starts a thread of discussion. Most newsreaders will have buttons for each of these options. As with listservs, it is a good idea to lurk on a newsgroup before you become an active member. To get an idea of what kinds of topics are appropriate, find out if the newsgroup has a **FAQ (frequently asked questions)** page. Newsgroup members will become irate if you post questions that are already discussed in the FAQ, and they will not appreciate messages that discuss topics beyond the scope of their news-group. If you make either of these mistakes, you could get flamed—bombarded with irate mail messages! (See Info Byte: Netiquette, page 32.)

Virtual Communities: Real-Time Communication

Real-time communication is different from the various forms of delayed communication that we have discussed so far—e-mail, listservs, and news-groups. In real time, your messages—whether text, audio, or video—are seen almost instantaneously by those on your channel, instead of being sent and read later by the recipient. There are two main methods of real-time communication—chat groups via **IRC (Internet Relay Chat)** and multiuser domains (MUDs, MOOs, MUSHs, etc.).

To participate in real-time communication, you need some special software. Chat groups, MUDs, MOOs, and videoconferences each require different software; sometimes, different software is even required from chat room to chat room, from MUD to MUD, and so on. This section provides an overview of some of the real-time communication options, as well as links to some Web sites to help you get started. And remember, the same netiquette (see page 32) for other forms of communication is still in effect in real time. For example, avoid shouting (addressing people in all caps), and be careful not to divulge too much personal information.

Internet Relay Chat

Internet Relay Chat (IRC) is a protocol that gives you the ability to commu-nicate in real time with people worldwide through **chat** groups. Once you have the proper software in place, you can connect to an IRC server. After you are connected to the server, you can sign on to one of the channels and communicate with others who are signed on to the same channel. You can have public conversation, where everyone on the channel is included, or a private conversation between you and one other person. Remember, though, that in IRC channels, the channel moderator can kick you off and refuse you future access, so follow netiquette (see page 32).

A good place to begin is with a document called The IRC Prelude, available at <http://www.irchelp.org/irchelp/>. Useful software that you can download is mIRC (a graphic client) at the address above, or LisztIRC at <www.liszt.com/chat/intro.html>. This page also provides IRC FAQs.

MUDs, MOOs, MUSHs, and WOOs

The first multiuser programming option was the **MUD (Multiuser Domain [Dimension, or Dungeon])**. A MUD is a computer program that creates a world for users to log on to (usually by Telnet). Users can participate in role playing, assuming various characters or personae. The next to come along were the **MOO (MUD Object-Oriented environment)** and the **MUSH (Multiuser Shared Hallucination)**. MOOs, MUSHs, and other multiuser domains are similar. They all have a gathering of users, usually role playing, but MOOs and MUSHs allow for physical objects to be placed in the virtual room where the participants are gathered. Among the latest in multiuser technology is the **WOO (Web Object-Oriented environment)**, where Web hypermedia capabilities are combined with MOO technology. These forms of real-time communication started out as ways to facilitate multiuser games. Now they are being used to create virtual societies. For beginner information, see the Megabyte University's Discussion List page at <http://www.daedalus.com/MBU/MBU.intro.html>. For more advanced information, see <www.csl.sony.co.jp/project/VS/index.html>.

A good place to get started with multiuser options is the Pueblo site at <http://www.chaco.com/pueblo/contents.html>. Pueblo is an example of client software needed to participate in virtual communities; this site also provides some general information and FAQs on multiuser communities.

Videoconferencing

Videoconferencing allows you and other people around the world who are signed on to the same conference, and who have the required audio and video software and hardware, to see and hear each other. You can also show each other images and text. One of the most popular software packages for videoconferencing is CU-SeeMe. For more information on videoconferencing, including CU-SeeMe and other software, go to <http://rocketcharged.com/cu-seeme/>.

File Transfer Protocol (FTP)

FTP (file transfer protocol) allows you to send or retrieve files from one computer to another. In reference to the Internet, it usually means downloading files (such as text files and software programs) from the Internet to your computer. You can download huge amounts of software for free or for a minimal charge at FTP archives, such as Shareware.com at <http://www. shareware.com>.

To download a file from an FTP archive, you need to log in with a user name and password. Most FTP archives use anonymous FTP, meaning that you use the word "anonymous" as your user name and your e-mail address as your password. Browsers equipped with FTP software will do this automatically, so that when you click on a file you want to download, it will begin downloading immediately.

The Internet provides a vast number of downloadable files, such as HTML editors (used for creating Web pages), chat software, graphics animators, games (including virtual reality), and screen savers. The easiest way to find these files is to go directly to a file archive, such as Shareware.com, where you can do a key word search, search the New Arrivals, or browse Most Popular Selections (the most often downloaded selections). Much of the software is free, called **freeware.** Some software, called **shareware,** requires a small fee. (Don't let Shareware.com's name fool you; most of its software is free.) In addition to Shareware.com, a good place to find software (as well as reviews and ratings of software) is ZDNet at <http://www.zdnet.com>.

You can search for other FTP archives by using the search engine Archie, but Archie is not as user friendly as most of the search engines discussed so far. With Archie, you need to know the name of the software for which you are looking. There is also a Web-based interface for using Archie, called ArchiePlex. You can find a list of ArchiePlex servers at <http://cuiwww.unige.ch/archie.html>. Even though ArchiePlex is Web-based, it is still rather difficult to use, so read the instructions carefully before beginning any searches.

Most graphic Web browsers, such as Netscape and Explorer, come equipped with FTP software. However, this software is usually restricted to downloading files and is not capable of sending files. In order to send files, you need full-service FTP software, which you can download for free. For the Macintosh, you can get Fetch at <http://www.dartmouth.edu/pages/softdev/fetch.html>, or, for a PC, you can get a free limited version of WS_FTP at <http://www.ipswitch.com/cgi/download_eval.pl?product=main>.

Risks and Precautions

The following section deals with some of the risks that you may encounter while working with the Internet. We also suggest some precautions that may help you avoid the most common pitfalls.

Privacy

It is not a good idea to put anything in an e-mail message that you would not want others to see, because messages can be intercepted or sent to the wrong person. Especially if the computer you are using (or your receiver is using) belongs to your school or employer, your messages are very easy for others to access. There are privacy programs available, but using such a program may make people suspect that something secret is going on.

If you turn your computer into a server, you can have problems with individuals being able to access documents and information on your machine other than what you want to publish.

Personal Security

Sometimes you may be asked to give personal information on the Internet, especially when downloading commercial software. Reputable businesses have taken precautions to ensure the security of the information you provide. However, if you are unsure of the vendor (or whenever you sign on to online news services), you should make a rule of giving just your first or last name and not giving your home address or phone number.

If you publish your own Web page (discussed in Chapter Four), be aware that your page is accessible to the public. You want to give careful consideration to the amount and kind of personal information that you post on your page, such as your picture, phone numbers, and addresses. It is one thing for the whole world to have your e-mail address; it may be quite another for the whole world to be able to recognize you on sight and drive to where you live.

Copyright

It is safe to assume that most of the material on the Internet is copyrighted. *The absence of a copyright notice does not mean that the material is not protected* or that it can be assumed to be in the public domain and therefore usable without seeking permission from the author or copyright holder. (For posting on the Web, however, the recommended procedure is to put "Copyright," the copyright symbol [©], the date published, the owner's name, and "All rights reserved" on documents that fall under copyright protection.) The only exception to using material from print sources that is protected by a copyright is "fair use," which usually means reproduction of a limited amount of material for educational purposes, criticism, comment, or news reporting. For more information on copyright issues, see <http://lcweb.loc.gov/copyright>.

Ideas, facts, titles, names, short phrases, and blank forms are not protected by copyright. Items in the public domain, such as government documents or items for which copyright has expired, are not protected by copyright and may be used without permission.

Libel

When someone knowingly spreads false information about another person, harming that person's reputation, or defaming them, it is called slander. However, when such information is published in print, it is defamatory writing and may be considered libelous. The same caution applies to writing published on the Web, so make sure that any information you post is true and verifiable. Libel is a crime and is punishable as a felony.

Plagiarism

For Web documents, you can create a link to someone's Web page, but *you may not* cut and paste any part of someone's Web page and place it on your own. Similarly, if you quote Web-page information in a written document, you must cite it properly. (See the section on documentation, starting on page 19.)

Viruses

Viruses can be devastating to your computer. They can damage or destroy both hardware and software. Viruses can get into your computer in several ways. One way is to put an infected disk into your computer's disk drive and open a file on it. Viruses can also be downloaded from the Internet when you transfer files to your computer—for example, by downloading software or text files. Viruses can also be sent via e-mail: Reading a message is not generally a problem, but if you open an attachment contaminated with a virus, your computer will become infected. Basically, if you do anything with e-mail beyond reading the message itself, your computer is susceptible to viruses.

You can use virus protection software to detect viruses and even prevent them from contaminating your computer. Some computers come with anti-virus software, but you can also purchase software or download it from the Internet. For the latest on computer viruses and anti-virus software, visit IBM's "Antivirus Online" at <http://www.av.ibm.com/current/FrontPage/>, the Federal Computer Incident Response Capability (FedCirc) site at <http://www.fedcirc.gov>, or the Department of Energy's Incident Advisory Capability site at <http://ciac.llnl.gov/>. At these sites, you will find information such as virus names, reviews of anti-virus software, and which viruses are currently at large.

Time Management

You can waste twenty-four hours a day, seven days a week, on the Internet if you are not careful. A good practice, therefore, is to separate "fun" Web sessions from "work" Web sessions. Determine before you begin a Web session which kind of session you intend it to be and how much time you can give to it. Then stick to your plans.

CHAPTER FOUR
FINDING INTERNSHIPS AND JOBS
ON THE INTERNET

When you start looking for internships or jobs, the Internet has searchable databases of job postings by employers worldwide. This use of the Internet is one of its fastest-growing areas and one that is especially important for students. Depending on the position you are looking for, you can search by type of job, key word, or your skills, and by city, state, or country.

Sites to Search for Jobs

With services like The Career Search Launch Pad at <http://www.pantos. org/cslp>, you can access several job-search engines. The Web pages available from the Launch Pad are Career Mosaic, NationJob, Online Career Center, and Net Temps. You can access these career-search engines directly from the Launch Pad Web page, or you can link directly to each of them, using the URLs given below. These are just a few of our favorite sites; you can find more on Mayfield's Web page at <http://www.mayfieldpub.com/ EnglishDepartment/resources/jobsinterns.htm>.

America's Job Bank <http://www.ajb.dni.us/>

Career Mosaic <http://www.careermosaic.com>

Monster.Com <http://www.monster.com>

NationJob <http://www.nationjob.com>

Online Career Center <http://www.occ.com>

Net Temps <http://www.net-temps.com>

Info Bit—Many of the job-finding services allow you to post your own résumé in their databank, which can make it easier for employers who are looking for someone with your unique blend of education and experiences. Usually, to post your résumé you will need to have a version written in HTML. The section on creating your own Web page (pages 41–43) will get you off to a good start in creating an HTML version of your résumé.

Internships
A great place to start looking for internships is Yahoo!'s Internships category at <http://dir.yahoo.com/Education/Career_and_Vocational/

Career_Planning/Internships/>. Some other listings are:

- Intern-Net
  http://www.InternshipPrograms.com/
- JobTrak
  http://www.jobtrak.com/
- JobWeb
  http://www.jobweb.org
- Princeton Review
  http://www.review.com/career/find/intern.cfm

You can also find internships listed on the Web under particular fields (such as journalism), or particular locations (such as Washington, D.C.), or with particular companies (simply find your target employer's Web page and search it for an internships section).

Scholarships

To find scholarship opportunities, go to Yahoo!'s scholarship site at <http://search.yahoo.com/search?p=scholarships>. Another good list may be found at <http://sandburg.unm.edu/>.

Creating Your Own Web Pages

To post your own Web pages, you first need to make sure that your ISP has the ability to house them. There is usually an extra fee to store Web pages, so check to see what the rates are. Once you have a place to store your pages, the next step is to learn HTML. HTML uses **tags** contained in angle brackets, < >, to mark up the text of your document. Basically, HTML tags act as a set of instructions for the Web browser (such as Netscape); the tags tell the browser how your Web page should look (what's bold, what's in color, where pictures go) and how to respond to mouse clicks and keyboard strokes (if someone clicks on a link, where the browser should take them, or what Web page or file you are linking to). If you are not familiar with HTML, there is an excellent tutorial (created by Eric Meyer for Case Western University) called "Introduction to HTML" at <http://www.cwru.edu/help/introHTML/>. Also, after you start working with HTML, it's a good idea to have a cheat sheet with all the HTML tags. For such a list, go to the Bare Bones Guide for HTML 4.0 (or the most current version) by Kevin Werbach at <http://werbach.com/barebones/>.

Guidelines for Web-page design. In many ways, good Web-page design follows the same principles as good page design in general—the document should be professional in appearance, important design elements should be used in a consistent way, and the document should be easy for readers to use (you can find more on how these principles apply to print pages in *Easy Access,* Second Edition, by Michael Keene and Katherine Adams, Mayfield, 1999). Here's how these principles apply to Web pages:

- **The document should be professional in appearance.** Chiefly, this means the page should not be cluttered. Think of your screen as being divided into, at most, three blocks, with each block holding a different kind of element (text, links, visuals). Keeping background ("wallpaper") material to a minimum also helps keep the page uncluttered. The major sections of the document itself should be indicated by headings, lists should be separated from text, and any data should be displayed in simple tables. Adding a link to your e-mail address and a "last updated" date are good finishing touches for giving your page a professional appearance.

- **Important design elements should be used in a consistent way.** "White space"—areas of the page in which nothing is printed—is critical to the design of print publications, and at least equally critical to Web-page design. The temptation for a newbie is to fill every pixel with colors and patterns. The logic, apparently, is, if there's any open space left at all, it's better to fill it with yet another dancing baby. But white space doesn't lie, and using lots of it in your Web page will really help the page's design. Use white space around the edges, at the tops and bottoms of screens, and especially between elements, whether vertical or horizontal. Instead of making long, endless pages, break text and graphics into shorter, linked pages. Try to stick with just one or two typefaces throughout, rather than seeing how many different ones you can use.

- **The document should be easy for readers to use.** Keep each Web page short, and keep your pages up-to-date. Especially on the "front" pages, try to shorten loading time by limiting visuals at least a little bit. When you do use images, try to keep the files small.

If you keep your Web pages uncluttered, use lots of white space, and make sure your pages load quickly, you're on your way to producing well-designed pages. Check your page on different machines and on different browsers to make sure that it looks the way you want it to. Also, remember that the information you are posting is available to anyone, so be careful what kind of personal information you post, such as pictures, phone numbers, and addresses (see "Personal Security," page 37).

Once you have your Web pages ready for the rest of the world, the final step is to make them available through search engines (such as Yahoo! or AltaVista). For other people to be able to look up your page with a search engine, you have to submit it. Of course it would be quite time consuming to submit your page to each search engine. To help make this task easier, sign up for a free trial account from Submit It! at <http://www.submitit.com>. Have fun!

Sending Your Résumé Electronically

If you have your résumé on the Web in HTML, prospective employers can view it and download it or print it out as needed. If you do not have your résumé in that form, you may be asked to e-mail it to a prospective employer. In that case, here are a few pointers to remember: E-mail programs today do not handle things like different type fonts or sizes, boldface type, or italics; and fancy spacing (centering, lists that use hanging indents, etc.) usually just contributes to a document that comes out on the other end in a mess. If there is a chance you will need to e-mail your résumé, you need a very plain version—one in which all headings are at the left margin, only one typeface is used (you can do some differentiation with uppercase letters, use asterisks instead of bullets, etc.), and, in general, all that fancy typography that makes your print or HTML résumé look so snazzy is gone. If you use a plain version, then your prospective employer just might get your résumé in an ungarbled form.

Putting your résumé into an attachment to a piece of e-mail is not a good idea, because there's no guarantee at all that the person receiving that attachment has a program to open it that will be compatible with the program you used to create it. You're better off just to paste your résumé right into the body of your e-mail. Finally, remember that once you e-mail your résumé to someone, chances are that person is going to enter it into an electronic database that holds thousands of résumés, so that individuals within the company looking for new hires with particular qualifications can let their computers search the database for the key words that name those skills. What key words can be found on your résumé, and are they the right ones?

CHAPTER FIVE
INTERNET RESOURCES

Reference Material

Dictionaries and Thesauruses
- Bartlett's Quotations (1901 ed.)
  http://www.bartleby.com/99
- Merriam Webster's Dictionary and Thesaurus
  http://www.m-w.com/home.htm
- Roget's Thesaurus (version 1.02)
  http://www.thesaurus.com
- Strunk's Elements of Style (1918 ed.)
  http://www.bartleby.com/141

Citations and Copyright
You can start with the copyright office at the Library of Congress <http://lcweb.loc.gov/copyright>, and then check "the copyright Web site" at <http://www.benedict.com>. There's a good discussion of citing sources at <http://libweb.sdsu.edu/cite.html>.

Libraries
- Internet Public Library
  http://ipl.org
- Library of Congress
  http://lcweb.loc.gov/library/

Newspapers
Nearly every large-city newspaper has some kind of Web presence now. Some are only small bits of the print newspapers, and others require either registration, or subscription for money, or both, for you to access them. Besides the lists available on Yahoo!, there's a good geographic listing at <http://www.newsrack.com>.

Broadcast News
- CNN
  http://www.cnn.com

- National Public Radio
  http://www.npr.org
- PBS
  http://www.pbs.org

News Filters
Try the combination of **news filter** and screen saver at <http://www.pointcast.com>

Book Reviews
- BookWire
  http://www.bookwire.com
- The Independent Reader
  http://www.independentreader.com

Online Writing Centers
There's a comprehensive list of these wonderful facilities at the National Writing Centers Association's home page <http://departments.colgate.edu/diw/NWCA.html>.

People Finders
Most of the major search engines have people finders (as well as Postal Service address finders, e-mail address finders, and phone number finders) available from their home page. For example, you can find Yahoo!'s people finder at <http://people.yahoo.com>.

Image Finders
It is becoming easier and easier to find particular images (pictures, paintings, images of any kind) on the Web, with the help of such pages as Mister Pix <http://www.mister-pix.com>, the AltaVista Photo Finder <http://www.altavista.com>, and the Yahoo! Image Surfer <http://ipix.yahoo.com>. If there is an image on the Web that you want to incorporate in a project, you can copy that image and save it to your computer. Once it is saved, you can put it on your Web page, put it in a word processing document, and the like. According to fair-use guidelines, a limited amount of copyrighted material may be used without permission for educational purposes, criticism, comment, or news reporting.

Here's how to grab images from the Web. To save an image, place your mouse over the image. If you are using a PC, hold down a right-click. If you are using a Macintosh, hold down a regular click. You will be given a pop-up menu. From the menu, choose "Save Image As." You will be given a box with options for a file name (be sure to keep the same extension if you change the file name, e.g., **.gif** or **.jpg**) and a file location (to put it in the folder and drive of your choice). Once the file is saved, you can open the image in a graphics program, such as Adobe Photoshop or Super Paint. You can choose to "Copy" it. You can then place the image in a word processing document. Once it is copied, open your word processor to the file where you want the image placed, and "Paste" it. If you want to place the image in a Web page, then save the image to the appropriate folder, and reference the file in the HTML file.

Remember: You should assume that just about everything on the Web is protected by copyright. Material does not have to have a copyright symbol on it to be so protected. Fair-use guidelines may be followed for use of copyrighted material without permission in student papers and projects.

CHAPTER SIX
SOCIOLOGY ON THE INTERNET

Introduction

While studying sociology, or while doing personal exploration, it is likely that you will encounter topics that you want to examine in detail. The Internet has become a powerful tool for locating the information that will answer your questions and provide such detail. This section, then, offers a guide to *begin* your search for information on the field of sociology and sociology topics on the Internet.

Sociology, like so many other disciplines, contains as many specific topics as there are sociologists. Researchers may be interested in topics such as class, gender, race, culture, environment, aging, medicine, and education. They also may be interested in combining topics—for example, studying how race affects the medical treatment a person receives, or how aging affects a woman's position in social class. The whole of human life, it seems, is tied to the study of sociology. An exhaustive list of Web sites that are relevant to the study of sociology might easily become a list of all of the Web sites and resources available on the Internet. Such a list would be nearly impossible to assemble and would be out of date almost as soon as it was published. More importantly, it would take the fun out of exploring the possibilities. However, what we can provide here is a guide to help you find Internet resources devoted specifically to sociology and the work of sociologists.

Sociologists wear many hats; they play many roles that help them explore the human patterns of behavior that interest them most. These roles can be combined under the following headings:

- Learners: Studying the ways in which sociology views both the world and the results of sociological work

- Researchers: Reading, working with, and using other research and data

- Participants: Applying sociological work in the real world and interacting with other sociologists

- Teachers: Passing their knowledge on to other sociologists and students of sociology

To some extent, this guide is organized around the first three roles. However, most of the Web sites listed on the following pages provide links to other sites devoted to specific research areas. We also have provided some tips on finding specific topics, including a guide to evaluating the Web sites you find, especially those that are not regulated by a professional organization.

General sociology references are listed first. This section contains sites that catalog links to other sociology Web sites. The next section, "Learning Basic Concepts of Sociology," provides a list of sites that may be helpful to students who are new to sociology and its theories of human behavior. The third section, "Using the Web for Sociology Research," provides links to journals, databases for articles and empirical data, and other sources of information that is important to working sociologists. The last section, "Participating in Sociology," lists virtual groups that have discussions on the Internet, and "in real life" (IRL) groups that meet to discuss sociology.

General Sociology Reference Sites

It is not difficult to find references to sociology on the Internet. The use of a search engine to find sociology, as described earlier, will yield an enormous number of Web sites. However, while exploring sociology you may want to find only general information. This section provides a list of Web sites that contain both general information on the discipline and links to other Web sites that also may be helpful.

- Research Resources for the Social Sciences
  <http://www.socsciresearch.com/>
- Julian Dierkes' Sociology Links at Princeton
  <http://www.princeton.edu/~sociolog/links.html>
- Social Science Hot List
  <http://www.yorku.ca/faculty/academic/ishwaran/hotlist.htm>
- SocioRealm
  <http://www.geocities.com/CollegePark/Quad/5889/index.htm>
- SocioSite: Going Dutch Sociology
  <http://www.pscw.uva.nl/sociosite/index.html>
- The SocioWeb <http://www.socioweb.com/~markbl/socioweb/>
- SocioWorld: Internet Resources for the Social Sciences
  <http://www.geocities.com/CollegePark/Library/8419/wbpthfnd.html>
- WWW Resources for Sociologists
  <http://osiris.colorado.edu/SOC/links.html>
- WWW Virtual Library: Sociology
  <http://www.mcmaster.ca/socscidocs/w3virtsoclib/index.htm>

Learning Basic Concepts of Sociology

Sociologists, like all scientists, are learning all the time. Sociology students, however, must begin with the basic concepts of sociology. The following sites on the Internet provide ample opportunity for rookies to become acquainted—and for veterans to become reacquainted—with the introductory teachings of sociology. The sites outline some of the major concepts in sociology and also provide links to sites where more detailed information is available. These Web sites provide a general overview of sociology and its elements. Some of them describe the work of theorists and the various concepts and terminology they contribute to the field.

Introduction to Sociology
The sites provided below introduce sociology to new students. They are wonderful sites for novices to explore the numerous concepts in sociology as well as to begin their exploration of sociology on the Internet.

- Sociology Cafe
  <http://www.sociologycafe.com>
- Sociological Tour Through Cyberspace
  <http://www.trinity.edu/~mkearl/index.html>

- GeoTeacher: General Sociology
  <http://home.att.net/~rmmwms/students/sociology.html>

Sociology Theories
One of the major elements in learning sociology is coming to grips with the theories and theorists that provide the concepts for study and use. The Web sites listed here are only a few of the many sites devoted to sociological theory. Some contain general information, whereas others contain information about specific theorists. Still others provide full text or excerpts from important social theories.

General Theory Sites
- Classical Sociological Theory
  <http://www.spc.uchicago.edu/ssr1/PRELIMS/theory.html>
- The Dead Sociologists' Society
  <http://www.runet.edu/~lridener/DSS/DEADSOC.HTML>
- A Sociology Timeline from 1600 by Ed Stephan
  <http://www.ac.wwu.edu/~stephan/timeline.html>
- SocioRealm: Social Theory
  <http://www.geocities.com/CollegePark/Quad/5889/socialth.htm>

- SocioSite: Sociologists
  <http://www.pscw.uva.nl/sociosite/TOPICS/Sociologists.html>
- Voice of the Shuttle: Web Page for Humanities Research
  <http://vos.ucsb.edu>

Specific Theorists and Their Works
- Addams, Jane
  Jane Addams <http://www.nobel.se/laureates/peace-1931.html>
- DuBois, W. E. B.
  The W. E. B. Dubois Virtual University
  <http://members.tripod.com/~Dubois/mont.htm>
- Durkheim, Émile
  The Durkheim Pages <http://granny.lang.uiuc.edu/durkheim>
- Gilman, Charlotte Perkins
  The "Yellow Wall-Paper" Site
  <http://www.cwrl.utexas.edu/~daniel/amlit/wallpaper/wallpaper.html>
- Marx, Karl
  The Marx/Engels Archive <http://csf.Colorado.EDU/psn/marx>
- Mead, George Herbert
  George's Page—The Mead Project Web site
  <http://paradigm.soci.brocku.ca/~lward/>

Academic Sociology Departments
Universities around the country offer diverse programs in sociology for both undergraduate and graduate degrees. Most offer programs that concentrate on providing students with a solid understanding of the art and science of sociology and helping students explore areas of personal interest. Other schools focus explicitly on some aspect of sociology (for example, social policy, race and ethnicity, or statistical analysis). For a detailed listing of these schools, use a search engine such as Yahoo!, or consult the Web sites provided in the "General Sociology Reference Sites" section.

The schools listed below are a sampling that represents different regions of the United States and different types of programs. The list illustrates the diverse array of programs offered by schools. Links to biographies of the faculty enable you to see the diversity of research interests and the many tasks required of sociologists in academia. On occasion, these Web sites also give you a glimpse into the social lives of sociologists, especially those of graduate students.

- **Wellesley College** <http://www.wellesley.edu/Sociology/intro.html>
- **Morehouse College** <http://www.morehouse.edu/soc.htm>
- **New York University**
  <http://www.nyu.edu/gsas/dept/socio/index.html>
- **Ohio University** <http://www.cas.ohiou.edu/socanth>
- **University of California at Berkeley** <http://sociology.berkeley.edu>
- **University of Illinois at Chicago**
  <http://www.uic.edu/depts/soci/index.html>
- **University of Michigan** <http://www.umich.edu/~socdept/>
- **University of Nebraska at Lincoln** <http://www.unl.edu/unlsoc>
- **University of Nevada, Las Vegas**
  <http://www.nscee.edu/unlv/Colleges/Liberal_Arts/Sociology>
- **University of Pennsylvania** <www.ssc.upenn.edu/soc/>

Using the Web for Sociology Research

The vast majority of a sociologist's work involves research. This research includes finding previously published material, collecting or finding previously collected data, and analyzing data. Many sites are available on the Internet to aid in this process, and these sites can be helpful to students of sociology.

Finding Sources

The work of other sociologists is priceless to the research process of a working sociologist. Previous work in an interest area not only illuminates the potential pitfalls, but it provides a foundation on which to build current research. Each piece of research is like a building block that adds its own dimension to our understanding of a topic.

Most articles need to be gathered from IRL sites such as libraries or archives. However, many people find it helpful to figure out what they'll be looking for and where to locate it before venturing forth. Sometimes looking at specific journal Web sites will help you locate information. At other times, the use of a database, library, or archive is more helpful.

Although many archives have yet to be catalogued and put on the Web, some libraries and databases of articles are available. The trick to accessing library Web sites is to use a search engine to search for a library that is physically near you (or one that you think will be helpful) or to call the library by telephone and ask if it has a Web site. Other useful research sites are listed here.

Online and/or Hard Copy Journals. Journals come from many different sources and address a variety of topics. Virtually every discipline has a plethora of journals that give voice to the research and ideas developed by practitioners. Sociology is no exception. Some journals focus on specific topics whereas others present a diverse collection of sociological research. Many Web sites for journals only give information about the journal and subscription information for the interested person to receive a hard copy version. Others, however, present the journal online, and users can access the contents electronically for free or for a small fee. The list below contains journals of each type.

American Journals
- *American Journal of Sociology*
  <http://www.journals.uchicago.edu/AJS/>
- *American Sociological Review* <http://www.pop.psu.edu/ASR/asr.htm>
- *The Honors Journal for and by Sociology Students of the World*
  <http://www.tryoung.com/journal-honors/undergradindex.html>
- *Journal of Contemporary Ethnography* <http://www.sagepub.com>
- *Social Psychology Quarterly* <http://www.u.arizona.edu/~spq/>
- *Teaching Sociology* <http://www.lemoyne.edu/ts/tsmain.html>

International Journals
- *The British Journal of Sociology* <http://www.lse.ac.uk/serials/bjs/>
- *The Canadian Journal of Sociology*
  <http://www.ualberta.ca/~cjscopy/cjs.html>
- *European Sociological Review* <http://www.oup.co.uk/eursej>
- *International Journal of Comparative Sociology*
  <http://www.yorku.ca/faculty/academic/ishwaran/ijcs.htm>
- *International Sociology*
  <http://www.sagepub.co.uk/journals/details/j0196.html>
- *Sociological Research* <http://kennedy.soc.surrey.ac.uk/socresonline/>

Available Databases of Articles. Many school libraries and local libraries are equipped with computer terminals that provide access to databases listing articles and their abstracts. These databases are priceless to the work of any researcher. Although many require fees to use and keep updated, some provide limited access for free (full access for a fee). The following two sites are good examples. Be aware that sites such as JSTOR may require permission to access their databases. For students and faculty this usually is provided through on-campus access to the Internet at a school; just type in the address. However, from off-campus terminals, or when you are using another Internet provider, you must find alternate ways of gaining access. One such method is the use of a **proxy server.** Your school's computer resource center should be able to provide you with the codes, passwords, and assistance to use a proxy server.

- CARL Uncover <http://uncweb.carl.org>
- JSTOR <www.jstor.org/journals>
- Cambridge Scientific Abstracts <http://www.socabs.org>

Online Libraries. Online libraries can provide a wealth of information, including access to the full texts of sources you may be seeking. Using online libraries such as the ones listed below is just like visiting your school or local library. The Web sites allow you to either browse their services or do detailed searches of their catalogs to ferret out the information you need.

- **The Library of Congress** <http://lcweb.loc.gov/> or <http://www.loc.gov>
- **Stanford University Digital Libraries Project** <http://diglib.stanford.edu/>
- **UC Berkeley Digital Library Project** <http://elib.cs.berkeley.edu/>
- **University of Illinois Digital Libraries Initiative** <http://dli.grainger.uiuc.edu>

Finding Data

Equally important for some projects is being able to peruse and use the data that other researchers have collected. Such research may contain the answers to questions that you want to explore, or it may provide data that you can use to explore specific topics. There are many sources of data on the Internet, although not all of them are free. The following list of Web sites may contain data that you can download for use. In addition, these sites may lead you to other sites that contain data for use or may provide contact information to obtain the data you seek.

- **Consortium for International Earth Science Information Network: Socioeconomic Data and Applications Center** <http://sedac.ciesin.org/>
- **Data on the Net: University of California at San Diego** <http://odwin.ucsd.edu/idata/>
- **FedStats (A one-stop-shopping site for federal statistics)** <http://www.fedstats.gov>

- **Integrated Public Use Microdata Series** <http://www.ipums.umn.edu>
- **Intra-university Consortium for Political and Social Research** <http://www.icpsr.umich.edu/index.html>
- **National Opinion Research Center** <http://www.norc.uchicago.edu/>
- **Population Index on the Web** <http://popindex.princeton.edu>
- **Social Science Data Archives: Europe** <http://www.nsd.uib.no/cessda/europe.html>
- **Social Science Data Archives: North America** <http://www.nsd.uib.no/cessda/namer.html>
- **Social Science Data Resources** <http://www.trinity.edu/~mkearl/data.html>
- **U.S. Census Bureau** <http://www.census.gov/>

Participating in Sociology

Participation occurs at many levels in the life of a working sociologist. The ideas and conclusions that sociologists gather may be applied in the real world, and thus their participation is exemplified in as many Web sites as there are groups that make use of sociological work. Keep in mind, as you find these sites on your own, the cautions provided in the section that follows, "Evaluating Web Sites."

Participation in sociology also means interacting with other sociologists. There are many forums in which this type of participation takes place. In real life, sociologists may listen to each other present their ideas at professional conferences or symposiums. Sociologists also may participate in online discussion groups through the use of newsgroups and listservs. The following links illustrate many of these forums. They are provided for you to explore the many ways sociologists interact with each other and with the world.

Application in the Real World
The list of organizations that make use of sociology in their everyday activities would be too long to list here. However, below are two sites that attempt to provide working models and resources for the use of sociology in the real world.

- **The New Social Worker Online** <http://www.socialworker.com/>
- **Praxis: Resources for Social and Economic Development** <http://caster.ssw.upenn.edu/~restes/praxis.html>

Professional Sociology Organizations

The following groups provide an open forum for discussion, critique, and brainstorming. They are instrumental in keeping the science of sociology alive and growing—by organizing meetings, publishing journals, and so on. These groups provide access to their many duties through Web sites designed to educate and create a sense of community. The sites are beneficial to students who wish to grasp the diversity and enormity of the discipline in different regions of the country, in the United States as a whole, and around the world—even for students who have no interest in joining the groups.

American Associations. The following Web sites are for organizations whose membership is primarily, but not restricted to, U.S. researchers. They traditionally hold their annual meetings in cities around the United States or in the regions which they serve.

• **American Sociological Association** <http://www.asanet.org/>
• **Eastern Sociological Society** <http://wings.buffalo.edu/ess/>
• **Mid-South Sociological Association**
  <http://www.uakron.edu/hefe/mssapage.html>
• **Mid-West Sociological Society** <http://www.drake.edu/MSS/>
• **North Central Sociological Association**
  <http://www2.hanover.edu/NCSA/>
• **The Pacific Sociologic Association** <http://www.csus.edu/psa/>
• **Progressive Sociologists Network** <http://csf.Colorado.EDU:80/psn/>
• **Rural Sociological Society** <http://RuralSociology.org>
• **The Society for Applied Sociology** <http://www.appliedsoc.org>
• **The Society for the Study of Social Problems**
  <http://itc.utk.edu/sssp>
• **The Society for the Study of Symbolic Interaction**
  <http://sun.soci.niu.edu/~sssi/>
• **The Southern Sociological Society**
  <http://www.msstate.edu/Org/SSS/sss.html>

International Associations. An exploration of sociology's roots will reveal that it is a discipline with strong ties to the works of social scientists in other countries. The work of scientists around the globe has always been important for the increasing knowledge of the discipline. Exploring the similarities and differences in the findings of sociologists who study social structures, cultures, and institutions in other countries, for instance, strengthens the overall scientific project. The following Web sites are a few examples of the many associations that exist outside of the United States.

* **Asia Pacific Sociological Association**
  <http://www.geocities.com/Athens/Cyprus/2004/>
* **British Sociological Association** <http://www.britsoc.org.uk>
* **Canadian Sociology and Anthropology Assocation**
  <http://artsci-ccwin.concordia.ca/socanth/csaa/csaa.html>
* **International Sociological Association**
  <http://www.ucm.es/OTROS/isa/>
* **Sociological Association of Aotearoa (New Zealand)**
  <http://saanz.science.org.nz>

Discussion Groups to Ask Questions and Stay Informed

Discussion groups, like professional organizations, provide sociologists and students of sociology with a venue in which to present and compare ideas, stay informed on current events in the discipline, and ask questions. This is especially informative for students of sociology when experts in the field survey ground-breaking ideas or rehash old arguments with new twists. Some discussion lists concentrate only on specific topics; others allow a broad range of discussion. Many more discussion groups exist than are listed here. However, as new ones develop and old ones disappear, users are informed through their communication in the other discussion groups.

Usenet Newsgroups. As discussed in Part Two, Usenet is a UNIX-based information system that maintains thousands of special-interest discussion groups (called newsgroups). Access to Usenet is provided through university computing accounts and other Internet service providers (ISPs). You should seek more information locally if you do not know how to access these resources.

Usenet newsgroup discussions differ from listservs (see below) in that messages are not sent directly to individual users, but are stored on servers for individual retrieval. Usenet newsgroups tend to be used by a much wider audience than individual listservs. The topics of messages can be extremely varied.

Some newsgroups spring up, die out, and are reborn with great frequency; others continue for long periods of time. It would be impossible to list all of the newsgroups that are of interest to sociology. Therefore, only a few of the sites are provided, to give you a general idea of what is available. Basically, if you want to talk about something, there is probably a newsgroup that has begun or is waiting to begin the discussion. To find lists of Usenet newsgroups (and some of them are searchable by topic), check out the Yahoo! search engine category on Usenet newsgroups for the most up-to-date list. Additionally, you can find a well-organized list of usenet newsgroups at the Usenet Info Center Launch Pad at http://meta-lab.unc.edu/usenet-i/.

One general-interest newsgroup is <alt.sci.sociology>. Here are some newsgroups for more focused interests.

Specific Interest
- soc.college
- soc.feminism
- soc.history
- soc.men
- soc.politics
- soc.religion.christian
- soc.religion.islam
- soc.rights.human
- soc.veterans

Cultural Discussion Groups
A more complete list (although, not an exhaustive one) of these types of sites can be found at Harvard University's William James Hall newsgroup Web site <http://wjh-www.harvard.edu/soc-sci/soc/news-soc.html>.

- soc.culture.african
- soc.culture.african.american
- soc.culture.arabic
- soc.culture.asian.american
- soc.culture.brazil
- soc.culture.british
- soc.culture.canada
- soc.culture.china
- soc.culture.french
- soc.culture.german
- soc.culture.indian
- soc.culture.iranian
- soc.culture.iraq
- soc.culture.italian
- soc.culture.japan
- soc.culture.jewish
- soc.culture.korean
- soc.culture.latin-american
- soc.culture.mexican
- soc.culture.misc
- soc.culture.peru
- soc.culture.polish
- soc.culture.portuguese
- soc.culture.scottish

- soc.culture.soviet
- soc.culture.spain
- soc.culture.swiss
- soc.culture.taiwan

- soc.culture.thai
- soc.culture.usa
- soc.culture.vietnamese

Listservs. Listservs are programs running on Internet servers that allow for the management of lists of e-mail addresses. These programs receive messages sent to the listserv's e-mail address and then immediately redistribute copies of that message to other addresses on the list. The effect is to create an electronic bulletin board on which messages can be posted and read by many users. Some lists can have thousands of members. Others will have only a dozen or so. Members can respond to messages either publicly (on the list) or privately (through a direct e-mail message). Traffic, or the rate at which new messages appear on the listserv, can range from one message a week to dozens a day. Listservs differ substantially from most Usenet newsgroups in that they are controlled by a "listowner," who has the ability to control access to subscriptions and monitor messages before they are posted. The listowner even has the power to delete any subscriber from the list. Listserv discussions tend to be much more professional than those in Usenet newsgroups. Most have open subscriptions, but some are exclusive, allowing subscriptions only from individuals with specific qualifications. It is always advisable to read all of the instructions and guidelines for the use of a specific list before posting a message.

On a well-maintained list, all messages should be clearly labeled. Some e-mail programs, such as Netscape Mail, Pegasus Mail, and Eudora Pro, will display messages with the same "Subject" line together as a thread, permitting users to read contributions to a discussion that may stretch over several days or weeks.

Some lists have advanced features that permit subscribers to specify the categories of messages that they would like to receive. Frivolous posts and requests that look as if you are trying to get someone else to do your homework are likely to be flamed with negative, mocking, or even insulting responses. Some lists are moderated by an individual or panel in an attempt to eliminate silly, useless, distracting, off-topic, or offensive messages. Most lists encourage new subscribers to lurk for a while in order to familiarize themselves with the level and kind of discussion in the listserv before contributing to the list. Try to get an idea of the kinds of participants and their personalities before jumping into a discussion. If you consider submitting a message to a listserv, remember that copies of it will go out to hundreds, if not thousands, of professors, potential colleagues, and employers.

The following are just a few of the dozens of sociology-related listservs on the Internet. To get involved with any of these groups, you must send an e-mail message to the address given. In the text section of your message, type only the command indicated.

- ABSLST-L, Association of Black Sociologists <listserv@cmuvm.csv.cmich.edu>: subscribe abslst-l [your name]
- CUSSNET, Computer Users in the Social Sciences <listserv@stat.com>: subscribe cussnet [your name]
- FAMLYSCI, Family Studies <listserv@ukcc.uky.edu>: subscribe famlysci [your name]
- INTERACT, Graduate Student of Symbolic Interaction <listproc@sun.soci.niu.edu>: subscribe interact [your name]
- MARXISM, Marxist Theory and Application <majordomo@majordomo.cc.jyu.fi>: subscribe marxism [your name]
- METHODS, Research Methodology in the Social Sciences <comserve@vm.its.rpi.edu>: subscribe methods [your name]
- PRAXIS, "Theory into Action" Discussion Group: Information can be found at: <http://wizard.ucr.edu/praxis/>
- SOCGRAD, Sociology Graduate Students <listserv@ucsd.edu>: subscribe socgrad [your name]
- The Sociological Omnibus Cafe (SOC) Discussion Group: Information can be found at: <http://cwolf.alaska.edu/~anlmg/soc/>
- SOCIOLOGY, General Sociology Discussions <listserv@thinknet.orange.ca.us>: subscribe sociology [your name]
- SOCIAL-THEORY, Discussion on Sociological Theory <mailbase@mailbase.ac.uk>: subscribe social-theory [your name]
- SSSITALK, Discussions on Symbolic Interaction <listproc@sun.soci.niu.edu>: subscribe sssitalk [your name]

A Few Words About Specific Topics

Most of the Web sites provided in this guide pertain to sociology in general instead of to specific research areas. However, the Internet offers an enormous number of sites devoted to specific topics of interest in sociology. To find the studies of your particular interest area, you can use any of the sites listed in the subsection, "General Sociology Reference Sites," and surf to find pertinent links. Or you can use a search engine such as Yahoo! to combine the key word *sociology* with your area of interest. Finally, you might also want to periodically check at *The Scout Report for the Social Sciences* at http://scout.cs.wisc.edu/report/socsci/current/index.html>.

As you surf, keep in mind that many Web sites are not regulated by a professional body, even if they are presented in a professional manner. For this reason, you should be careful about accepting at face value all of the statements you find on the Web. However, there are a few professionally regulated Web sites that can help you find information. One of these is the American Sociological Association.

American Sociological Association Sections
Provided below are a few of the Web sites for topical sections of the American Sociological Association. These may prove helpful in your search for information on your own interest areas.

- **Collective Behavior and Social Movements Section**
  <http://www.u.arizona.edu/~jearl/cbsm.html>
- **The Community Web: Community and Urban Section**
  <http://www.urbsoc.org/community/>
- **Comparative-Historical Section**
  <http://www.sla.purdue.edu/academic/soc/comphist/>
- **Culture Section** <http://www.newcollege.usf.edu/culture>
- **Environment and Technology Section**
  <http://csf.colorado.edu/orgs/roschke/es/env.html>
- **Section on International Migrations**
  <http://www.ssc.msu.edu/~intermig/>
- **Marxist Sociology Section**
  <http://csf.colorado.edu/psn/marxist-sociology/index.html>
- **Mathematical Sociology Section**
  <http://www.sscnet.ucla.edu/soc/groups/mathsoc/mathsoc.htm>
- **Medical Sociology Section**
  <http://www.kent.edu/sociology/asamedsoc/>
- **Section on Organizations, Occupations, and Work**
  <http://www.northpark.edu/acad/soc/oow/>
- **Section on Peace, War and Social Conflict**
  <http://www.la.utexas.edu/research/pwasa/index.htm>

- **Section on the Political Economy of the World System**
  <http://www.cas.vt.edu/pews/index.html>
- **Social Psychology Section** <http://burkep.libarts.wsu.edu/SPNews/>

Evaluating Web Sites[1]

Another way to locate sites that contribute to your understanding of a particular topic is to simply eliminate sociology from the key word search on a search engine and explore what people outside of sociology have to say about the subject area. However, you must bear in mind that as you explore the Internet you will find Web sites created by individuals, groups, and institutions that may or may not be experts on the topic. It will be up to you to assess the validity of the information you find. I suggest that you consider carefully the following criteria.

Who Produces the Web Site. Who produces the information is very important to assessing the quality of information on a Web site. Everybody who produces information has an agenda. The person's priority may be to educate, to sell something, to spread propaganda, or to gain supporters. Knowing who the person or group is can help you evaluate the information presented.

Check the names of organizations listed as sponsors, contributors, or producers, and consider what the organization does. Look also for brief introductions to organizations on home pages. Web-site creators know that Internet users often stumble into Web sites while surfing, and they often treat the home page as an advertisement to introduce themselves and/or the groups they represent.

Some groups and individuals belong to broader communities that have shared ethical and behavior standards that restrict the information that the members provide. The URL may provide a clue about whether the Web-site owner belongs to such a broader community. For instance, consider the URL extensions ".gov" and ".edu," which refer to governmental and educational Web-site owners. You can expect government sites to provide information in accordance with specific standards, rules, and laws that apply to the presentation of material. You would not be likely to find personal editorials on a government Web site. Likewise, creators of educational sites may be expected to adhere to the regulations and norms of

---

1. Source: Gongaware, Timothy B. (G. Speigelberg, technical advisor). 1998. "Appendix B: Searching the Internet: A Brief Introduction to Researching Sociological Topic Areas" in Amanda Konradi and Martha Schmidt. *Reading Between the Lines: Toward an Understanding of Current Social Problems.* Mountain View, CA: Mayfield Publishing Co.

their specific academic communities. They may, for instance, be required to have any work presented on a Web site reviewed by a panel of peers. People and groups who create Web sites using other extensions (".org," ".com," ".net," and so on) may not be restricted in what they present or how they present it.

Why a Web Site Is Presenting Information. The agenda of a person or group will also influence the information presented. Thus, determining why a group is presenting information is the next important factor for assessing the quality of information you find. There are two ways to review the objectives of a Web site: Examine the layout of the site and look at the organization's mission statement.

First, look at the layout of a Web site's home page. The links it provides to information within the Web site can give you clues to the objectives of its owners. For instance, the home page of the National Urban League, or NUL <http://www.nul.org>, offers links to information about the organization; topics such as "About the National Urban League," "Departments," "Urban League Affiliates," and "Resources and Programs" let you explore what the organization does and what it offers. By contrast, the National Association for the Advancement of Colored People, or NAACP <http://www.naacp.org>, initially presents links that lead you to information about positions the organization has taken on recent events. A smaller group of links located at the bottom of the home page leads you to information about the organization. The differences in these layouts indicate that NUL places a priority on conveying information about itself and its services, whereas the NAACP is more concerned with conveying information about its position on specific issues. This conclusion is consistent with the official objectives, found in "About the NUL" and "About the NAACP."

The information page (or Mission Statement link) tells you the goals and objectives of the organization, and the means it uses to achieve its mission. The mission of the NUL is to "assist African Americans in the achievement of social and economic equality . . . through advocacy, bridge building, program services and research." The NAACP, on the other hand "relies on the press, the petition, the ballot and the courts . . . to ensure the political, educational, social and economic equality of minority group citizens of the United States." The first noticeable difference between these two groups is the way in which they describe how they reach their objectives. NUL uses program services and research to obtain its goals, whereas NAACP uses "the ballot and the courts." A second difference is in the objectives of the groups. Whereas NUL concentrates on "social and economic equality," NAACP adds political and educational equality. Perhaps most importantly, the two groups represent slightly different populations. NUL officially concentrates on assisting African Americans, whereas NAACP officially extends its resources to all "minority group citizens of the United States."

These two pieces of information, the layout and mission statement, are valuable for assessing the nature of the organization and why the group has chosen to present its views. You should be able to determine from the information given on the home page and in the mission statement if the group is concerned primarily with doing research, creating policy, or selling something. Every organization will provide you with an easy way to join the group, because every organization needs to increase its membership. Research groups need financial support to continue their research. Policy groups need public support to convince government agencies to make or change policy. Commercial groups need buyers for their products. Remember that the way a group presents its claims and its methods is intended to entice you to join its mission. Be aware, then, that most organizations will present themselves in the best possible manner and usually will omit negative information.

What Is Being Presented. The last important step in assessing the information presented on a Web site is to look at what the organization is presenting. Sociologists traditionally draw upon the work of others and make use of published sources that can be verified. Many sociology journals publish only work that has been positively reviewed by a group of peers. Professionals therefore trust that any claims made in the journals' articles are based on research conforming to particular scientific standards. The peer review works as a safeguard to keep professional sociologists truthful in the claims they make. The Internet has no such safeguard. There is no single person or committee that reviews the information presented on a Web site, so any claim can be made regardless of the truth.

Many Web-site papers do not contain bibliographies or well-documented sources. Read any papers very carefully, noting the conclusions the Web-site owners draw. Identify how the group is backing up its facts. Note if the information is simply the Web-site owner's opinion. Note if it draws upon an organization's own research, the research of affiliated organizations, or other independent sources. One question to keep in mind is: Could I verify the sources of all of the information presented if I had to?

Also, examine the information for one-sided points of view. Some organizations are vehement advocates for specific populations, whereas others are advocates for any group. Those that take only one group of people as their focus will invariably make use of information to their benefit and may ignore other sources of information that they deem detrimental to their cause. It is therefore important to look for any indicators that a group may be one-sided.

Take for instance the Web sites for the Knights of the Ku Klux Klan, or KKK <http://www.kukluxklan.org>, and the American Civil Liberties Union, ACLU <http://www.aclu.org>. Right up front, the KKK's site provides a link to "Our Vision" where the group states that "we are promoters of White Christian Civilization. We believe that the concepts of private property, free enterprise, representative government, parental rights, freedom of speech, right to trial by jury, right to address the government for a redress of grievances, etc. are essential ingredients for a civilized and moral society." This statement implies that information presented and used by the KKK will be filtered through a Western Christian belief system geared toward defending this single belief system against all others. Likewise, the ACLU's Web site states that its mission "is to assure that the Bill of Rights are preserved for each new generation." This is also a single belief system, and the mission of the ACLU also implies that information presented will be filtered through a bias toward its own belief system. The critical difference between the two statements is that although the KKK officially consists of "White Christian men and women," the ACLU extends its commitment and membership "to all people regardless of race, sex, religion, national origin, sexual orientation, age, physical handicap, or other such classification." Thus, the ACLU will be somewhat more inclusive of other points of view in the information it uses and presents.

A Sphere of Democracy. Anyone who has the right access can create a Web site. If the person is not part of a broader professional organization, he or she does not need to have the Web site reviewed by anyone. Therefore, the claims made may or may not be worthwhile information. It falls to you, the researcher, to assess the Web-site creator's process of inquiry and the conclusions drawn. In this regard, the Internet has become a bastion for democracy, where freedom of opinion and speech reign supreme. The price for this freedom, as it is in democracies outside of the Internet, is that individuals must critically address the information they obtain, and must use the information responsibly.

INTERNET GLOSSARY

applet   See **Java**.

Archie   A search engine for FTP archives.

ArchiePlex   Web-based interface for using Archie.

ASCII   The basic code e-mail uses; does not allow underlining, italics, etc.

bandwidth   The amount of information that can be transferred across a network at one time.

bit   The smallest unit of information in a computer; represented by 0 or 1; eight bits equal a **byte**.

Bookmark   A tool provided by most Web browsers that enables you to save Web page URLs so that you can return to them at any time.

Boolean logic   A system for searching a database that uses the operators AND, OR, and NOT to look for two variables.

bps (bits per second)   A measure of data transmission capacity, used to describe a modem's speed, such as 28.8 Kbps (or 28,800 bits per second).

browser   An interface for reading information on the World Wide Web, either graphic (such as Netscape or Explorer) or text-only (such as Lynx).

bulletin board (BBS)   Area where users can read and post messages as well as download files.

byte   A unit of information in a computer, equal to 8 bits.

cache   A region of memory where frequently accessed files can be stored for rapid retrieval.

CD-ROM (compact disc, read-only memory)   A compact disk used to store and retrieve computer data.

chat   Electronic conversations among Internet users taking place in real time in chat areas (or chat channels, groups, rooms, or sites).

client   The computer and software you use to access Internet servers.

DNS (domain name system)   The convention for translating the names of hosts into Internet address; see also **URL**.

domain name   The part of the Internet address (URL) that specifies the area on a computer reserved for a particular organization, such as `mayfieldpub.com`. In this example, `.com` stands for "commercial"; other types of organization designations include `.edu` for "educational" and `.gov` for "governmental."

download   To transfer information from one computer to another, or to transfer information from a network to your computer.

e-mail   Electronic mail, one of the most popular uses of the Internet, it can be sent to an individual or a list.

FAQ (frequently asked questions)   Lists of common questions about a particular product, service, or topic.

file path   Subdirectory in a URL, leading to the specific file you want.

flaming   Sending a large number of angry messages, usually to someone who has broken the rules of netiquette.

freeware   Software you get for free.

FTP (file transfer protocol)   The standard protocol for transferring files across the Internet. Most browsers have one-way FTP; for two-way (the ability to send as well as receive), you can acquire FTP software for both Macintoshes (Fetch) and PCs (WS_FTP).

gateway   A device whose purpose is to aid in the transfer of packets of information from one network to another.

GIF (graphics interchange format)   File format for images that are viewable on the Web; see also **JPEG**.

Gopher   A menu-driven information system created at the University of Minnesota.

hits   The number of times a particular page is accessed, or the number of successful matches you receive during a key word search.

home page   The main, or starting, page for a series of Web pages.

HTML (hypertext markup language)   The formatting language of the World Wide Web.

HTTP (hypertext transfer protocol)   The protocol for reading HTML programs from the Web.

hyperlink   See **link**.

hypermedia   Links among various kinds of multimedia objects, such as video, audio, and virtual reality, in addition to text and graphics.

hypertext   A text link that takes you to another file on the Internet. A hypertext document contains hypertext, or hyperlinks, or both.

Internet   A global network of linked computers; home to the World Wide Web, newsgroups, bulletin boards, Gopher, and online forums.

IRC (Internet relay chat)   See **chat**.

ISP (Internet service provider)   A company that provides subscribers access to the Internet.

Java   Programmed mini-applications ("applets") for Web browsers.

JPEG or **JPG (joint photographic expert group)**   File format for images that are viewable on the Web; see also **GIF**.

Jughead   A search engine for Gopher document titles.

link   Short for **hyperlink**. A link, text or graphic, that takes you to another file on the Internet or another location in a document.

listserv   A program that distributes e-mail to a mailing list.

lurk   To browse and read messages, but not actively participate in a discussion group. A good idea before joining discussion groups.

mailing list   A discussion group that shares an interest in a particular topic; messages sent by members of the group are e-mailed to all its members.

megabyte (MB)   A unit of computer information storage capacity equal to 1,048,576 bytes.

modem   A device that allows a remote computer to communicate via phone lines to networks and other computers.

MOO (MUD object-oriented environment)   Multiple-user environment based on object-oriented programming technology. See **MUD.**

MUD (multiuser domain [dungeon, dimension])   Virtual environment on the Internet primarily used for role-playing games such as Dungeons and Dragons.

MUSH (multiuser shared hallucination)   A MUD variation.

netiquette   Etiquette on the Internet; the guidelines for preferred behavior when communicating with others on the Internet.

network   A system of computers that can transmit information from one to another.

newbie   Someone new to the Web.

news filter   A software program that lets you customize your news. You can choose what type of news you want and from what source.

newsgroup   A discussion group, or informal bulletin board, that shares an interest in a particular topic; newsgroups are located on Usenet, where articles are read and posted.

packet   When information is transferred from the Internet to your computer, it is broken into packets, or pieces, which are transmitted to your computer and reassembled by TCP software.

page   Any Web document viewable with a browser.

platform   The operating system that your computer runs—for example, DOS (disk operating system), Windows, or Macintosh.

POP (post office protocol)   The standard protocol for reading Internet mail sent using SMTP.

portal   A Web page that combines search engine, subject tree, news filter, etc. Most major search engines now have first pages that are actually portals.

protocol   Information format. The protocol lets two computers know what type of information is being transferred. The protocol for transferring information across the Internet is given in the first part of the URL (e.g., http, ftp, gopher, telnet).

RAM (random access memory)   The amount of available short-term memory in a computer directly correlating to the speed of your processor—the more RAM you have, the faster your computer is.

real-time communication   Communication in which your messages are seen instantly; makes possible "live" conversations.

ROM (read-only memory)   The unchangeable portion of the computer's memory containing the start-up instructions for your system.

route   The path a packet takes from the server to the client.

search engine   A program that allows you to perform key word searches to locate Web documents.

server   A computer accessible to other networked computers.

shareware   Copyrighted software that is distributed on a trial basis; you eventually have to pay for it if you want to continue to use it beyond the trial period. The cost is generally minimal.

SMTP (simple mail transfer protocol)   The standard protocol for transferring e-mail from one computer to another across the Internet.

spam   Unsolicited e-mail usually sent to a large number of users, such as to a Usenet group or a listserv mailing list.

subject tree   A hierarchical directory of information.

surfing   Aimlessly exploring the Internet by clicking links from one page to another.

tags   Codes used in **HTML** (hypertext markup language).

TCP/IP (transmission control protocol/Internet protocol)   TCP is the software your computer uses to create an interface with the Internet. TCP software receives the packets of data transmitted across the Internet and reassembles the corresponding file so that you can view the resulting Web page. IP is the protocol that computers use to talk to each other on the Internet, and it helps to define the route packets take.

Telnet   A standard protocol for logging on to another computer remotely. For example, if you want to log on from home to your UNIX account at school, you can use Telnet.

thread   The original newsgroup message (article) and all of its associated replies.

UNIX   A freeware computer operating system used by many colleges and universities.

URL (uniform resource locator)   An address for an Internet location.

Usenet   A UNIX-based computing system used mainly for discussion and newsgroups.

Veronica   A program that searches the full text of Gopher documents.

videoconference   Two or more people interacting through real-time video and audio feeds.

virus   A self-replicating destructive program that can be downloaded from the Internet or obtained via an infected file on a diskette. A few viruses are harmless and even amusing, but most can destroy the data on your hard disk.

Web page   A document accessible on the Web.

World Wide Web   The segment of the Internet that uses primarily HTTP.

WOO (Web object-oriented environment)   A virtual space primarily used for role playing similar to MUD, but located on the World Wide Web.

INDEX